Praise for *The Quiet Burn*

"Lynn is a powerhouse. I can't think of anyone better to offer guidance on how to build resilience at the same time as achieving your personal and professional ambitions. At a time of great complexity in the workplace, this book is much needed."

—Anna Jones, CEO of the Telegraph Media Group

"Quite obviously, every woman in the workforce should read this book. Lynn offers an important lesson that every successful woman learns along the way: You must preserve your body and soul, even as you expend every energy to reach your goals. And if you ignore this warning, your body will eventually offer a painful lesson to make the message clear. Reading this book and heeding its advice could save you from a costly detour in your career—and in your life."

—Terry Savage, nationally syndicated financial columnist for the *Chicago Tribune*

"This is a manifesto for all women. I loved the combination of empathy, real case studies, and practical exercises packaged up into an easy flow that felt truly authentic, not preachy, and hitting the issues head-on."

—Jayne Fieldhouse, head of marketing and communications at Royal Bank of Canada Global Asset Management

"Lynn Blades doesn't just offer a guide with *The Quiet Burn*—she issues a wake-up call. This book is a master class in self-awareness, resilience, and the power of embracing your truth. It dares you to confront reality, harness your strengths, and reignite your soul with purpose and passion. More than that, it's a call to action for women to unite, support one another, and drive the transformative change the world so desperately needs."

—Jo Crawford-Boyle, chief marketing officer at Bang & Olufsen

"The power of Lynn's message comes from her authenticity. Staying true to her principles, morals, and unwavering self-belief, Lynn offers powerful examples of overcoming the barriers built from prejudice and ignorance. Through humility, honesty, and passion, she shares her personal journey in a way that is relatable and believable while also inspiring and achievable."

—Ruth Whitby, chair of general practice at Cleveland Clinic, London

"Your health is your number-one wealth, and *The Quiet Burn* is a brilliant book that keeps this mantra front and center. It will nourish your soul and give you that supportive hand on your back and permission to pause, reflect, and breathe. Thank you, Lynn, for this book and for reminding us to go at our own pace and to remember self-care."

—Karen Blackett, CBE, chancellor of the University of Portsmouth and former president of WPP UK

"Lynn challenges the outdated narrative that we must sacrifice ourselves on the altar of success, offering instead a powerful road map for sustainable achievement. This book is essential reading for every woman who's ever felt the quiet burn of trying to do it all, and a wake-up call to organizations about the true cost of burnout. *The Quiet Burn* isn't just timely—it's urgent and necessary. This book will be a lifeline for women who appear to be handling it all while silently burning out."

—Viviane Paxinos, CEO of AllBright

"Lynn Blades is a force. This book is a guide and companion for women who get it wrong while striving to get everything right. I can relate to her wisdom and guidance—and can't recommend this book enough to those who want it all."

—Debbie Wosskow, OBE, entrepreneur and cochair of the Invest in Women Taskforce

THE QUIET BURN

THE QUIET BURN

The Ambitious Woman's Guide to Recognizing and Preventing Burnout

LYNN BLADES

Fast Company Press

The author's opinions expressed herein are based on her personal experiences, observations, and research and readings on the subject matter. The author's opinions may not be universally applicable to all people in all circumstances. The information presented in this book is in no way intended as a substitute for spiritual, medical, psychological, legal, or other professional counseling. The publisher and author disclaim liability for any negative or other medical, psychological, or other outcomes that may occur as a result of acting on or not acting on anything set forth in this publication and the related website, workbook, or presentation.

Fast Company Press
New York, New York
www.fastcompanypress.com

Copyright © 2025 Lynn Blades

All rights reserved.

Thank you for purchasing an authorized edition of this book and for complying with copyright law. No part of this book may be reproduced, stored in a retrieval system, or transmitted by any means, electronic, mechanical, photocopying, recording, or otherwise, without written permission from the copyright holder.

This work is being published under the Fast Company Press imprint by an exclusive arrangement with *Fast Company*. *Fast Company* and the *Fast Company* logo are registered trademarks of Mansueto Ventures, LLC. The Fast Company Press logo is a wholly owned trademark of Mansueto Ventures, LLC.

Distributed by Greenleaf Book Group

For ordering information or special discounts for bulk purchases, please contact Greenleaf Book Group at PO Box 91869, Austin, TX 78709, 512.891.6100.

Design and composition by Greenleaf Book Group
Cover design by Greenleaf Book Group

Publisher's Cataloging-in-Publication data is available.

Print ISBN: 978-1-63908-130-1

eBook ISBN: 978-1-63908-131-8

To offset the number of trees consumed in the printing of our books, Greenleaf donates a portion of the proceeds from each printing to the Arbor Day Foundation. Greenleaf Book Group has replaced over 50,000 trees since 2007.

Printed in the United States of America on acid-free paper

25 26 27 28 29 30 31   10 9 8 7 6 5 4 3 2 1

First Edition

To my incredible parents, the architects of my foundation, built on love, integrity, and self-belief—pillars that have empowered me to construct a life of purpose and resilience

To all the inspiring women who shared their stories with me, allowing others to learn from their experiences

You are a force for good.
You are a force for change.
You are a force to be reckoned with.

Contents

Preface: Hear Me Out ix
Introduction: Be the Change 1

Part One: Is That Smoke on Your Horizon? 5
  1: Land of the Burnt 7
  2: Superwoman 37
  3: Where There's Smoke, There's Danger 61
  4: From Imposter to Formidable Force 81

Part Two: Looking Out for Number One 107
  5: Self-Care 109
  6: Self-Criticism 129
  7: Self-Compassion 151

Part Three: A Phoenix Rises from the Ashes 177
  8: Rebirth 179

  Conclusion 207
  About the Author 213

PREFACE

Hear Me Out

I envision a day when women embrace their power, recognizing their value to society and their potential to bring about change. I dream of a future where class, gender, and race no longer serve as barriers.

This dream is not exclusive to women. Achieving it requires a collective effort, including support from those in positions of power, particularly White men. Although I may not witness the complete realization of this dream in my lifetime, I maintain a sense of hope.

The time for change is now. If women unite and collaborate, we can become a formidable force. It's time to demand immediate action and tangible results. We must establish a strong foundation, stand together, and be the change we want to see in this world.

However, the pursuit of true equality often takes a back seat in the hustle of daily life. We are constantly on the move, rarely taking a moment to acknowledge our accomplishments. Consequently, we miss out on developing a strong sense of self-worth and pride. When was the last time you paused to reflect on your own happiness? Think about it. That long? Damn.

On a daily basis, I encounter remarkable women who are caught up in their own relentless pursuits, trapped in a cycle that lacks clear direction or purpose. They find themselves in a never-ending loop of slaving hard at work, often to find themselves hitting the glass ceiling, and then returning home to run a household and nurture a family, either on their own or with a partner. Either way, the balance of responsibility lies squarely on a woman's shoulders. At some point it inevitably becomes difficult to maintain this cycle without personal consequences. How can women stay in the game when they are uncertain of their destination or the reason behind their journey? This is at the heart of why women are leaving business at an alarming rate. They are exhausted and burned out.

The metaphor of burnt toast encapsulates the plight that many of us women face. Everyone knows what it's like to pop a freshly cut piece of bread into the toaster, only to have left it

Preface: Hear Me Out

long enough to get a bit too crisp. Often we'll salvage that piece of toast by scraping of the burnt part and covering it with a bit of butter and jam. Now, imagine that instead of putting a fresh piece of bread in the toaster, you started with the burnt one every day, and every day you attempted to salvage that piece of toast until you simply could not. Like burnt toast, we risk becoming scorched crumbs, mere remnants of our true potential.

We women have been conditioned to prioritize the needs of others over our own—from the workplace to the home. When I think of my greatest role model—my mother—I'm inspired by her selflessness. Her day began at 5 a.m. as she prepared for work at the CIA, but not before she made breakfast for her three children and packed their lunches. She headed to work with dreams of advancing from the secretarial pool to a role that challenged her intellect and potential. After a full day, she returned home by 6 p.m., picked us up from our after-school activities, prepared dinner, and often helped with homework. Just writing about her schedule leaves me exhausted.

She maintained that routine until we were old enough to help ourselves. My father, likewise, is an incredible individual who devoted himself to ensuring our family's well-being. His role was to fulfill his potential to provide opportunities for us all to excel. This was his primary focus, and his responsibilities, while significant, were less physically and emotionally demanding. Don't get me wrong—they both knocked themselves out because that's what Black people had to do in the 1960s to make it. However, my point is, this same societal structure of male and female roles has shifted very slowly over the last five decades, something that became alarming clear during COVID-19.

Burnout is a debilitating force that slowly erodes every aspect of your life, often without your awareness. This societal conditioning runs deep, disregarding and marginalizing women—not the future I envision for you, myself, or our daughters.

However, it does not have to be an inevitable fate; it is a path we frequently unknowingly choose. We women have been conditioned to neglect our own needs. This mindset deceives us into believing we can handle anything when, in reality, these efforts can leave us drained and hollow.

I've witnessed this pattern of behavior every day in my own life and in the lives of the women I work with as an executive coach. For two decades, I've worked with women ranging from global heads in Fortune 500 and Fortune 100 companies, to entrepreneurs running their own businesses, as well as ambitious women filled with aspirations. All these women face daunting challenges in balancing successful lives while often neglecting accountability for their own well-being. It is a cycle I am determined to break.

But where do we start? Self-care is merely the initial step. We must take action to bridge the gap between recognition (we have a problem) and implementation (here's how to fix it). Authentic self-care commences when we actively prioritize our well-being.

Mindfulness is not merely a passing trend; it is a timeless practice of self-honoring that has been neglected in our fast-paced lives. It involves asserting our worth, something women often underestimate. We dilute our needs, fearing rejection or believing our desires to be unreasonable.

I have a vivid memory of a female client, an equity partner at a prominent law firm who brings in millions and earns a high six-figure salary. She hesitated to request the firm sponsor her on a wellness retreat because she felt the need to prove herself further. This situation perplexed me. Why would someone who contributes so much to their firm feel unworthy of a small investment?

This mindset, in which even valuable contributors believe they must constantly earn what should already be rightfully theirs, exposes a systemic flaw in how we perceive self-worth and entitlement in professional settings.

This distorted mentality is widespread, particularly among women in positions of power. They often believe they need to give more to deserve what they want. Yet do male executives hesitate to ask for company sponsorships or make trade-offs for their development?

THE QUIET BURN

No.

We must be direct in expressing our needs. If we don't voice our requests, they are likely to go unmet. This fear goes beyond mere rejection; it's about how being denied makes us feel.

The sense of rejection is a mechanism intended to hinder our progress, preventing us from claiming what we have earned, embracing our achievements, and recognizing our worth.

Confidence and self-respect are evident when we believe in our values. That's why we need to start acting as if we deserve success. Instead of doubting ourselves, we should confidently assert, "Why not me?"

We bring as much, if not more, to the table and deserve recognition.

Without our contributions, not only individual projects but the entire world would suffer.

The world will fail without great women, and this trajectory is at risk if we don't prioritize self-care.

The essence of our impact lies in the solidarity of sisterhood.

Together, our collective resilience can become the cornerstone of global change.

It is astonishing to observe the limited progress that has been made since my time as a young journalist at WBBM TV in Chicago, where I endured racism and sexual harassment and was made to feel like my ambition was futile. How could I

Preface: Hear Me Out

forget being in my early twenties, proudly walking through the halls of a CBS network television station only to be belittled by the beloved anchorman patting my behind. Most days I had some reporter, producer, or anchor hurling some kind of sexist bullshit in my direction. That was simply the status quo.

Yes, change is occurring, but at a sluggish pace. It seems that numerous men in influential positions are now, albeit somewhat hesitantly, beginning to recognize and address the changing dynamics surrounding them, often exhibiting noticeable unease.

The ongoing issue of women being underpaid in the workplace perplexes and frustrates me. Why do American women earn eighty-seven cents to every dollar and British women eighty-two pence to every pound? This makes my blood boil.

Something is very wrong when it is estimated that it will take over one hundred years to balance this equation. Say what?

Women need to speak more openly about money. It's not a dirty word. It is power. Without equal pay, we don't have equal power.

In top leadership circles across the globe, particularly where men dominate, there is a noticeable failure to address gender equality with urgency. It is a blind spot, a deeply ingrained bias brought on by the homogenous composition of the top structures of power. Men simply undervalue the significant role that women play in propelling organizations and society forward.

THE QUIET BURN

Confronting this issue is not merely about fairness; it is critical for fostering growth and nurturing creativity. While efforts have been made to increase diversity at lower levels, the higher one ascends, the more representation dwindles. In my opinion, there is no valid justification for this disparity. The meagre number of women leading major corporations today is discouraging. I would have expected to witness substantial, fundamental changes occurring since my graduation from Dartmouth College in 1982.

The data speaks for itself. In 2024, 10.4 percent of Fortune 500 companies are led by women. Women heading Global 500 companies is 5.6 percent, a drop from the previous year. Furthermore, in 2024, women control $31.8 trillion in worldwide spending, and it is estimated that women will control 75 percent of worldwide discretionary spending in the next five years.[1] So why aren't more of us sitting at the top table across industries, given those statistics? The progress we anticipated simply does not exist. Fear seems to be a driving force behind much of it. While

---

1 Emma Hinchliffe and Joey Abrams, "The Share of Fortune 500 Businesses Run by Women Can't Seem to Budge Beyond 10%," *Fortune*, June 4, 2024, https://fortune.com/2024/06/04/share-of-fortune-500-businesses-run-by-women/; Emma Hinchliffe and Nina Ajemian, "The Share of Women Running Global 500 Companies Falls to Just 5.6%," *Fortune*, August 5, 2024, https://fortune.com/2024/08/05/the-share-of-women-running-global-500-companies-falls-to-just-5-6/; NielsenIQ, "Shaping Success: A Deep Dive into Women's Impact on the CPG Landscape," April 4, 2024, https://nielseniq.com/global/en/insights/analysis/2024/shaping-success-a-deep-dive-into-womens-impact-on-the-cpg-landscape/.

Preface: Hear Me Out

there are now more diverse faces in corporations, the profound, transformative change we desperately need remains elusive.

Women in positions of power still doubt their rightful place and capabilities. People from marginalized communities question why doors are being opened for them instead of seizing these opportunities without hesitation. This deep-rooted issue permeates our culture and society. To achieve genuine progress, one must disregard doubts, trust their instincts, and follow their aspirations. This is about ensuring diversity, equity, inclusion, and equal opportunities for all.

I strongly support affirmative action, a (now almost entirely defunct) proposition that opened doors for me and so many others like me with the goal of creating equal opportunities for women and underrepresented people, recognizing the lasting effects of momentous historical injustices. These measures are necessary for fostering genuine progress and enabling individuals to achieve their full potential.

In a society where stakes are high, such as in a burning house, there is an instinctive tendency to prioritize the rescue of White males over women and people from Black or ethnic communities. They are immediately perceived as owners and recognizable figures. This response is deeply ingrained in a survival instinct.

If it were my house on fire, my priority would be to rescue my daughter. I have raised her to be a formidable force in her own right. She possesses sharp intellect, holds a master's degree in anthropology, and works as a journalist, offering a unique perspective. She represents a new wave of thought and a vision for the future, something we desperately need. She is an agent of change. This is why I am particularly drawn to empowering young talents who lack certain privileges, helping them develop leadership skills and realize their potential as architects of the future.

Despite being aware of the additional hurdles I have faced and the extra effort I have had to put in to achieve what I have, I do not feel jaded at my age. I have been cheated and denied opportunities because I am a Black woman living in an unwelcoming landscape. However, this awareness does not dampen my optimism. My commitment to progress remains unwavering, regardless of the obstacles. Until my last breath, I will strive to ensure that our workforce reflects the diversity of our world.

This conviction is of utmost importance. Many individuals, especially women, face fatigue and burnout. We are tired of being unheard, of being invisible, of missed opportunities, of our ideas being appropriated, and of our worth being underestimated.

In a burning building, I choose to save a woman, because they are often overlooked and unseen. In a world filled with challenges, my priority lies in empowering individuals whose potential goes unnoticed, especially women, the ultimate embodiment of EQ (emotional intelligence) and IQ. I recognize their potential as future leaders who can rise to the highest ranks and pave the way for others.

The world needs more trailblazing women, such as Oprah Winfrey, Michelle Obama, Madeleine Albright, Sheryl Sandberg, and Isabel Wilkerson to pave the way. It is beyond question that if women were afforded the same opportunities as men, the world would undergo and experience a remarkable transformation.

INTRODUCTION

Be the Change

People of every race possess inherent goodness and a genuine desire for change. However, the power structures that govern society remain largely homogeneous: same gender, same race, same or similar backgrounds. It is imperative that those of us outside this homogeneity infiltrate these structures, even though those structures often recoil and fortify themselves when the status quo is threatened.

Injustices pervade the lives of women, people from different races, cultures, classes—essentially anyone who identifies differently from a White, middle-class male. We are not demanding grand gestures of reparation. All we seek is a fair chance to level the playing field.

This message holds immense significance at this moment.

THE QUIET BURN

Though not a novel concept, capturing people's attention has always proven arduous. I prefer candidly expressing my thoughts and opinions, as I am frankly exhausted, and diplomacy is not my top priority.

I can navigate seamlessly between Buckingham Palace and Watts; my adaptability knows no bounds. I have comfortably existed in both realms and can assimilate into any environment. Many of us, myself included, recognize that we could thrive in any setting if given the opportunity.

When I inform my female clients, ranging from high-finance professionals to media executives, that they resemble burnt toast, they immediately understand. They are depleted, fully aware of their exhaustion. This sentiment applies to a diverse range of individuals, including the woman who adeptly manages a six-figure household with the same finesse as a business, all while raising her family, yet remains fully recognized for her contributions.

These are the people I address—a diverse group of women who are fatigued from being undervalued, unheard, burdened with excessive stress, and expected to effortlessly juggle everything, which is of course an unrealistic expectation.

Allow me to pose a question: Among you, who can truthfully say they are content with their lives? Has anyone achieved everything they aspire to?

This is a call to action.

Introduction: Be the Change

My aspiration is for this book to herald a new chapter in your life, centered around the themes of self-respect, rejuvenation, reinvention, resilience, and self-love.

I will try, in these pages, to validate your instincts, and teach you not to overlook them. If nothing else, I hope this book will assure you that you are not alone in this struggle. I want to empower you to make better choices, find your voice, and understand that you deserve the best.

Life involves compromises, but you should not compromise your well-being. Jobs come and go, and while failures teach us valuable lessons, sacrificing your health is not a sustainable solution.

My role is to advise, not to persuade. I can offer you guidance, but the choice to follow it is yours.

My confidence in this book's value comes from knowing that the message will resonate with many readers. My work with countless women has shown me that there is always someone in the room who will connect with these words. My aim here is not to focus on just one group of readers, but to speak to a broader audience, to anyone ready to listen and make a change. That includes the good male ally.

I want to leave you with the belief that *you are a force for good, you are a force for change, and you are a force to be reckoned with.*

This book offers some of the wisdom I have been able to

gather on living a fulfilling life, respecting yourself, effectively communicating your needs, and recognizing the peril of ignoring your personal well-being.

As you read this book, don't simply skim the pages. Let the words sink in, and reflect on them. Do the exercises I've presented throughout the book. Commit to living a life without the quiet burn.

PART ONE

Is That Smoke on Your Horizon?

CHAPTER 1

Land of the Burnt

Imagine standing in a landscape ravaged by fire, surrounded by thick smoke, and engulfed in darkness. Once-majestic trees are reduced to mere ashes, serving as a stark reminder of desolation. Your vision is limited to a short, hazy radius. This scene reflects an internal battle where hope is absent, and the path forward is obscured by uncertainty. Rebuilding a life from these ashes feels like trying to grasp nothingness—an almost impossible task, as everything crumbles into more ash. Utter hopelessness consumes you, leaving you overwhelmed and gasping for each breath, struggling to make sense of your surroundings.

Those who have experienced the most profound impact of burnout know the soul-crushing weight it carries. Fear clings to you, and you yearn for a way out. How do you navigate a sea of ash when there is no solid ground beneath you? Everything feels unstable and impermanent. Trapped in isolation, helplessness, and deep sadness, escape seems unattainable.

This desolation manifests in various ways, physically, mentally, and emotionally. Mood swings, sleep issues, forgetfulness, muscle tension, anxiety, lack of focus—all take their toll. Yet, amid the darkness, stories emerge of people rising from the ashes like the mythical phoenix. Even in the bleakest times, a flicker of hope persists, though it may seem impossibly distant. I'm here to assure you that finding a path to a new reality is possible.

"Superwoman" Syndrome

During the 1980s, society propagated the notion of a "Superwoman" syndrome, portraying a woman who seemingly had it all—a thriving career, a perfect family life, and the remarkable ability to balance motherhood, marriage, and ambition flawlessly.

But let's face the truth—this highly idealized Superwoman is nothing more than a myth. Chasing after this illusion is a perilous game. It is unrealistic and frankly absurd to believe that one can do it all: flawlessly execute all these responsibilities, maintain their well-being, and find true happiness.

This pursuit is akin to running on an endless treadmill. You may be moving, but you are far from being truly present. Life becomes a monotonous routine where your eyes are open but you fail to truly see. You blindly race forward with no end in sight, perpetually carrying the burden but never reaching the finish line.

In a race like this, you are the horse, not the rider. It is not you who walks away with the trophy or the prize money, it is the rider—your company or your boss who gets the win. It feels like an unrelenting cycle of galloping, training, and being pushed to improve. But for what purpose? You do not receive the credit you rightfully deserve.

Perhaps you know someone like this in your workplace. (Perhaps it's you.) She embodies the Superwoman mentality to a tee. She never seeks help, burdening herself with everyone else's work, unable to say no, and avoiding conflict to maintain her "team player" image. She works tirelessly, yet all she receives is a mere pat on the back.

She is constantly overlooked for recognition or promotion because she is too busy being everyone's go-to person for unloading tasks. Unaware of the systemic cycle she has entangled herself in, her contributions go unrecognized. Ironically, the very qualities that make her an invaluable asset are what render her invisible when it comes to acknowledgment and advancement in her career.

Consider this a wake-up call. It is time to let go of the Superwoman facade and start asking, "Why not me?" Embrace your accomplishments and confidently step into the spotlight.

You are not merely a participant in this race—you have every right to lead it.

Two Faces of Darkness

When you begin your mornings without motivation to face the day, a shadow of darkness descends. The temptation to stay under the covers is strong, but you gather the strength to get up and go through the motions.

Indifference toward your appearance or performance becomes the norm. You manage to make it to work, but your mood is clouded by irritability, leaving you feeling out of control. Feelings of rejection and unfulfillment start to creep in as if no one is truly listening to you. In the back of your mind, you might even consider leaving your job.

But practical worries soon take hold. Concerns about bills, school fees, and rent or mortgage payments cause hesitation. You convince yourself that life isn't so bad, that you need this job, and fear starts to tighten its grip.

This fear becomes a barrier, disrupting your sleep and lingering in your subconscious, leaving you with a persistent feeling that something is amiss. But then you wake up, and your focus narrows down to the bare necessities of survival.

Lost in this cycle is the power to shape your own destiny. Fear is a natural instinct, and the fight-or-flight response takes a strong hold. Finding comfort in routine makes the idea of change seem daunting. You settle, telling yourself that receiving a paycheck is enough.

What you may not realize is that your lack of engagement is not going unnoticed by your boss. Someone is keeping track of the fact that you're not fully present. It's a situation where if you don't initiate change, someone else might decide for you, potentially leaving you in a precarious position.

It's a vicious cycle that is incredibly difficult to break free from. Sleeplessness, difficulty concentrating, memory lapses, and anxiety become constant companions. Even love feels like a burdensome weight, as every aspect of existence bears down heavily on you. You're devoid of any sense of accomplishment or fulfilment.

The imperative to prioritize your own happiness and well-being has been lost. You've become disconnected from recognizing and cherishing your own happiness, caught up in solving everyone else's problems instead of focusing on your own needs.

Then we encounter women who brim with ambition, stay laser-focused on their goals, and continuously chase success and financial rewards. Their darkness looks different. In their relentless pursuit, they often neglect their own mental, emotional, and physical well-being, paying a steep price. Despite getting tantalizingly close to their goals, they watch someone else snatch the prize at the last moment.

In their unyielding chase, they miss out on vital aspects of life, losing sight of the value of balance and the bigger picture. Their determination is commendable, but their tunnel vision misleads them, obscuring the human element and the need for a comprehensive strategy. Fixated on their goals, they forget to consider the broader perspective.

This hunt for success ultimately leads to burnout; realizing that their hard-fought goals remain out of reach is a devastating blow. All that effort, sacrifice, and toil—and for what?

Even upon reaching their goals, they are confronted with a deep sense of emptiness when they realize that the price they paid for material gains was their soul. This realization usually dawns too late, and they've already traded their soul for a place at the top.

Ladies, it is time to open your eyes.

We often settle into routines, conditioned to accept less than what we truly desire. Hoping for spontaneous improvement is a dangerous myth; real change requires action. The illusion that perseverance alone will make things better must be dispelled.

True improvement only comes when you actively stand up, strategize, and take control of your destiny.

Remember, neglecting your physical, emotional, and mental well-being will inevitably lead to burnout. You do not need to reach a point of utter exhaustion to take action. The key is intervention at the first sign of imbalance.

Getting past Overwhelm

Feeling overwhelmed is akin to having your boundaries blurred. It occurs when you are bombarded with responsibilities, challenges, and expectations that drain your energy. Saying no becomes an insurmountable burden, and before you know it, you find yourself engulfed in a deluge of tasks. You're trapped because you haven't set limits; you haven't said no. Instead, you've attempted to juggle everything and everyone simultaneously.

This results in a complete loss of focus, even though you believe you're doing the right thing. But for whom are you truly doing it? Certainly not for yourself. You may assume you can handle it, but is it truly living when you feel suffocated, as if there's an oppressive weight bearing down on you? When you're burdened with worries, tasks, ambitions, and the fear of others, your aspirations, happiness, and needs become lost in the chaos.

The constant pressure depletes your energy, leaving you

feeling unstable and trapped. You expend effort trying to move forward, but it's as if you're running in place. You're weighed down, losing your momentum. Your drive and determination seem to fade away.

Perhaps you've heard someone say, "I've lost the will to live," and maybe you've even experienced it yourself. Breaking free from this requires the courage to pause. To rediscover your motivation, remind yourself that life happens. Reassure yourself that this challenging phase is just that—a phase. Harness the power of gratitude by thinking about the good health of your friends and family and then prioritizing self-care. Actively take steps to move forward, knowing that this too shall pass.

Feeling overwhelmed often serves as a clear indicator of underlying anxiety. Shortness of breath, panic attacks, lack of motivation, fatigue, restlessness, and difficulties in focusing—these symptoms manifest alongside physical ailments such as aches and pains. Stress, particularly its impact on breathing, can manifest in various ways.

Feeling overwhelmed at work often stems from a lack of clear boundaries and difficulty saying no. The power of saying no should not be underestimated. It's crucial to evaluate whether you can realistically take on a request and if it falls within your responsibilities. While teamwork is important, especially during crises, there is a risk of others taking advantage of your willingness to help, especially if they perceive you as someone who won't assert themselves. It's often easier to go along with the majority rather than face potential conflict, even when "no" is the right answer, but "yes" slips out instead.

This issue is particularly common among women who find it challenging to refuse requests. Pushing yourself constantly without adequate breaks can lead to decreased efficiency and performance. It's a slippery slope toward burnout, a state you should strive to avoid at all costs.

Exercise Challenge: Find Your Power in Saying No

It is disheartening to witness how easily women prioritize the needs of others while neglecting their own, oblivious to the repercussions. Therefore, allow me to offer some advice on harnessing the power of one of my favorite words: *no*.

Tap into Your Values

Saying no becomes easier when we align with our values and trust our intuition. Research shows that living by our values promotes our health and well-being.[2] If a request conflicts

---

[2] For example, see Agnieszka Bojanowska, Lukasz D. Kaczmarek, Beata Urbanska, and Malwina Puchalska, "Acting on Values: A Novel Intervention Enhancing Hedonic and Eudaimonic Well-Being," *Journal of Happiness Studies* 23, no. 8 (2022): 3889–3908.

with our values, it's a value incongruence. By staying true to our values, we can kindly decline with a simple "no." When leading a project and asked to help with another task, consider the impact on your time and on the quality of the project. Politely decline.

Separate the Request from the Relationship

Declining a request can feel like rejecting the person, not just the request. This misconception creates pressure to always be a "good person" to avoid hurting others or damaging relationships. But saying no to a request is not rejecting the individual. Understanding this lets us prioritize our well-being without fearing hurt feelings.

Saying No Without Saying the Word "No"

We can decline a request without using the word "no." Instead, we can use alternative statements that convey the same message politely. For instance, consider using phrases like these:

- "I would love to attend, but unfortunately, I have prior commitments."
- "Currently, I don't have the availability."
- "Thank you for the invitation, but I am not available."

It's easy to effectively communicate a negative response without explicitly using the word "no."

Look at What You'll Gain by Saying No
Instead of fixating on what you might lose by saying no, take a moment to reflect on what you stand to gain. It's all too common for our minds to gravitate toward the negative, such as the fear of missing out, when faced with a decision. However, we have the power to shift our focus to the positive—what we will gain by "missing out"—which can make saying no a little easier.

Consider the Personal Cost of Saying Yes
When someone makes a request, they are seeking something from us. However, it's important to recognize that fulfilling that request comes with a cost. Understanding the value of what you're sacrificing by saying yes empowers you to confidently say no when needed.

Choose Being Respected over Being Popular
Although saying no may result in a temporary loss of popularity, it is often accompanied by a gain in respect. By declining certain requests, you demonstrate that you value your time, assert your self-worth, and prioritize what is best for you.

Be Clear Rather Than Vague and Noncommittal

Sometimes, we soften the impact of saying no by giving vague responses. We might say things like, "I'll do my best to come," or, "I'll try to get out of work early." But when we respond this way without intending to go, we put the other person in a worse position. Being noncommittal only prolongs the inevitable no, making it harder for both parties involved.

Getting over Burnout

Recovering from burnout is often more intricate and prolonged than expected. It's not simply a matter of taking a short break and expecting to bounce back fully.

Burnout deeply affects your mental, emotional, and physical well-being, necessitating a comprehensive and intentional approach to healing. This process entails not only resting but also reevaluating your work-life balance, establishing stronger boundaries, and often seeking support.

The path to recovering from burnout necessitates reconnecting with your personal needs and values. It's a transformative journey toward rediscovering a healthier and more fulfilling way of living.

Desolate

Desolation is feeling disconnected and isolated from others. You might be interacting with other people, but these interactions are all shallow and barely hinting at your need for support. You might maintain a facade of strength, but it's a fake front because you have no one to share your innermost thoughts and feelings with.

Putting on this mask is exhausting. It's similar to a pressure constantly building, threatening to erupt without warning. This unpredictability adds a layer of danger, as you are never quite sure when the facade will crumble.

It's a silent struggle, like a ticking time bomb of emotional and mental strain, leaving you perpetually on edge, wary of the moment when the pressure becomes too much to bear and uncertain as to what will happen if that time bomb explodes.

Maxine's Story

Let me tell you about my client Max.[3] She's an experienced food enthusiast and a marketing maven, driven by her love for everything edible. Beyond being the mastermind behind Women in the Food Industry, a charitable organization empowering women, she is also a highly regarded expert in her field.

---

[3] To protect the privacy of my clients, most of their names have been changed.

I was entrusted with supporting Max during a challenging phase in her career, as she grappled with burnout while serving as the head of marketing at Great British Chefs. Despite feeling overwhelmed, easily provoked, and undeniably exhausted, Max remained stalwart in the face of the emotional turmoil she was experiencing.

"I felt like I was working very long hours, and yet I'd have a member of my staff who was not pulling her weight and was undermining the rest of the team, which made me feel like even more was on my shoulders," she explained.[4]

This scenario depicts the quintessential narrative of entrepreneurial burnout. The organization boasted a staff of only five seasoned members along with an overabundance of inexperienced newcomers and a dearth of HR support. Yet as the flames of stress consumed Max, she soldiered on, ignoring the telltale signs of burnout for a while. Believing that an imminent sale of the company loomed overhead, Max selflessly sacrificed herself to ensure the business appeared market-ready—until the truth became obvious and unbearable.

Max recalled those stressful days. "I'd be working throughout the weekend and late at night just to get my work done. We would spend so much time either in meetings about strategy

---

[4] Maxine, interview by the author, October 9, 2024, London. All other quotations from Maxine in this chapter come from this interview.

or meetings about our selling, as well as having appraisals and interviews and taking on new staff and planning—then I would start crying in the toilets. . . . I wouldn't have said it was burnout. I just felt angry, tired, and annoyed. I thought to myself that unless I get help with the HR side, I can't keep doing this. It's not good for me. I just felt like I wasn't being supported."

To make matters worse, Max felt further isolated by being middle-aged and menopausal. She told me, "You feel like you're being gaslighted, and you're being too emotional. It wasn't just me that was feeling like this—another woman was going through a similar situation and felt that they weren't listening to her as well. The male partners felt that we were taking the situation too personally and that we were being too emotional about it all. That was 100 percent because we're women; they would never say that to any of the guys."

Eventually, it all became overwhelming. There were too many chefs in the kitchen, and no one was extinguishing the flames. She described her turning point this way:

> I went to the office one day, and people were leaving left, right, and center because they felt that we weren't going to sell. They felt that they wanted to get out before we went under. I just burst into tears. I don't usually cry. . . . I might

have cried in front of my boss once before when he was shouting at me, but I don't think I even did that. . . . I thought I was going to walk, like walk . . . well, probably down the block or something, but he physically pulled me back. People don't quite understand that it's not as easy as just leaving because you've invested like seven years of your life, and it is complicated. . . . You're feeling that you're getting a pot of gold at the end of this imaginary rainbow, [and you] don't want the pot of gold to be snatched away . . . when you're so close to it. Then you say, "No, I've got to carry on."

Max did carry on, but not for long. Brexit damaged the company's sales prospects, and Max left to gain some perspective, focus on self-care, and take charge of her own destiny.

The Pitfalls of Silence

Staying silent about your struggles leads to a deepening sense of solitude. It is a lonely road to constantly strive for unattainable perfection and try to fit into the mold of society's notion of Superwoman.

When we are asked, "How are you?," our immediate response is often, "I'm fine," even when that may not be the case. It has become customary in our society to conceal our true emotions and reply with a standard, superficial answer.

What if we defied expectations and honestly expressed our genuine feelings? What if we were open and transparent about our emotions? We all know that being truthful about our emotions can help us create profound personal connections.

Displaying vulnerability is one of the most effective ways to establish deeper and more intimate relationships. Never mistake vulnerability for weakness. It requires strength and resilience to embrace—and admit—your vulnerability, and the rewards in terms of instant rapport and deeper connections are certainly worth it.

You have to heed the signals your body and mind send you. Ignoring these signs and pretending to be engaged when you are not truly present might work for a while, but this response will prove unsustainable.

You will stay alone and isolated if you don't share your feelings. You become merely a vessel, burdened with this negative energy, exhausting yourself as you work to keep up a false exterior.

Nourishing Your Soul

The essence of the soul thrives on nourishment. When we neglect our soul, it withers, losing its curiosity, connection, and openness to love.

To nourish the soul, we must strike a balance between introspection and engagement. This entails embracing vulnerability, sharing our experiences, and engaging in meaningful communication.

Feeling soulless is like being in an office, watching others connect and flourish while we feel disconnected, numb, and unsure why we're not part of the group. We question our emotional state, wondering why we swing between overwhelming numbness and overpowering emotions. These extremes are our instinctual fight-or-flight responses. We may feel overwhelmed, as if we're treading water in a sea of challenges while others sail along smoothly.

Hiding our struggles is merely a temporary solution. Eventually the strain becomes evident. We must heed the warning signs early, before they intensify and consume us in the relentless inferno of stress, leaving us without respite or a way to extinguish the growing flames.

This escalation can not only cause personal anguish but also have a visible impact on our work performance and relationships. How do we heed the warning signs?

Land of the Burnt

To avoid the inferno, be vigilant and detect the faintest whiff of smoke.

We often notice small sparks of problems emerging, but all too often, we hope these issues will resolve themselves. We think, "This too shall pass."

However, is it realistic to expect these sparks to extinguish on their own? The stark truth is, they won't. Left unattended, they will smolder and seethe until they transform into small flames, growing into a raging fire. We have to be proactive and douse them as soon as we feel them growing inside us.

Such self-awareness is crucial not only for our survival but also for caring for our inner being. It means tuning in to our deepest needs and addressing them. It means nourishing the health of our soul, which will in turn ensure our long-term emotional and psychological resilience.

The feeling of bleakness, especially in a professional environment, often arises from a deep-rooted sense of constantly being overlooked and undervalued. It's frustrating to witness male counterparts effortlessly ascending the career ladder while you, equipped with similar ambitions and skills, struggle to reach those same rungs. And let us not forget those women who are only out for themselves, who would happily climb over you to get to the top under the misconception that there is only room for one of us at the top table. That's an ill-conceived notion created by entitled White men and propagated by self-serving women. As the late, great Madeleine Albright said, "There is a special place in Hell for women who don't help each other."[5]

This ongoing battle can distort your perspective, making you feel like you've lost control of your own path, as if the reins of your destiny have slipped from your grasp and are being held by those who don't understand your worth.

This is soul-destroying and it intensifies the sense of injustice and disparity in your professional journey. You can't work in that kind of atmosphere.

Hopelessness seeps in when you find yourself stagnant or overwhelmed in pursuing your goals, which is akin to being aboard a runaway train. It's reminiscent of the saying, "Be careful what you wish for because you just might get it."

Instead, strive for a balance that not only caters to your personal needs but also fosters your well-being and happiness. This balance should ultimately lead to a fulfilling life for you and a positive impact on those around you.

Set Priorities

There are times when we all find ourselves off-kilter, but recognizing and acknowledging these moments can empower us to

---

[5] Madeleine Albright, *Hell and Other Destinations: A 21st-Century Memoir* (Harper, 2020), 279.

initiate change. However, we often choose to ignore the warning signs and end up pushing ourselves to the brink of burnout.

Yet it's important to accept that having it all, all the time—basically, being Superwoman—is an unattainable ideal. We have to pick and choose; we have to say no, speak up for ourselves, and put those things first that mean the most to us.

When it comes to feeling a sense of clarity about our goals and our life, prioritization beats multitasking by a mile. I'm not a proponent of continuously juggling tasks unless it's an absolute last resort. The benefit of prioritizing, which includes making tough choices, is that it allows you to focus on what's most important and will ultimately enhance the quality of your life.

Women are growing increasingly weary of tirelessly chasing societal standards without receiving fair returns. The cumulative effect of feeling unheard, unappreciated, and underpaid takes its toll. Many women find themselves operating on autopilot, stuck in the landscape of burnout, often without even realizing it. They failed to heed the warning signs that they were close to that inferno. While autopilot may seem like a means of self-preservation, it ultimately leads to a numbed existence rather than a truly fulfilling one.

This state becomes a trap that stifles our true potential. We might feel fear when we acknowledge when something is amiss, but we have to feel that fear and do it anyway.

Growing from the Ashes

To break free from the cycle of self-denial and self-neglect, you must first learn to recognize the tell-tale signs of that cycle. It is often easier and more convenient to turn a blind eye to the signs rather than confront issues head-on. However, this avoidance can lead to detrimental consequences, including failing to achieve your highest potential.

How can we recognize when we're caught in a destructive behavior pattern? For me, it used to be impulse buying. Many of you likely relate to destressing by purchasing items you neither need nor truly want, squandering your hard-earned money. I know from experience that breaking this habit is challenging, and sometimes it doesn't happen until you're broke! Other indicators of destructive behavior include:

- *Self-harm:* This is a profound and serious form of self-destructive behavior where individuals intentionally injure themselves. It can be a way to manage overwhelming emotions, express feelings that seem impossible to put into words, or feel a sense of control over their pain. It's vital to acknowledge the seriousness of self-harm and provide empathetic support alongside professional help to those in need.

- *Volatility:* This volatile type of anger can erupt in destructive outbursts, sparked by even minor frustrations or misunderstandings. Imagine a situation where intense reactions lead to shouting, throwing objects, or even physical aggression. These moments of fury can cause deep emotional distress for everyone involved and are likely to harm relationships.

- *A sense of despair:* Experiencing a deep sense of despair about the future can drastically shape our outlook on life. This overwhelming hopelessness might arise from personal setbacks, mental health struggles, or societal challenges. When we're caught in a cycle of negativity, believing that things can't get better, it often leads to self-destructive behaviors as a coping mechanism. Recognizing these feelings and reaching out for support are pivotal steps toward reclaiming hope and embarking on a journey of healing.
- *Addiction:* Compulsive or addictive behaviors, such as excessive gambling, substance abuse, or binge eating, can be significant indicators of self-destructive behavior. These actions often serve as coping mechanisms to deal with underlying emotional issues or stress, ultimately leading to further harm if not addressed.
- *Assigning blame:* Blaming, criticizing, and defensiveness are like relationship kryptonite, chipping away at the safety and trust we all crave. When one partner plays the blame

game, tension and distrust quickly take center stage. Criticizing doesn't just hit self-esteem hard; it shuts down open conversations. And defensiveness? It blocks conflict resolution, spinning us into a negativity cycle that's tough to escape. Over time, these habits can erode the bedrock of trust and intimacy, making it a real challenge to keep a healthy, supportive connection intact.

- *Emotional instability:* Picture a rollercoaster of emotions, where mood swings, anxiety, and irritability can make every day feel unpredictable. These rapid emotional shifts can challenge one's ability to maintain steady relationships or manage stress. Minor triggers can set off a whirlwind of feelings, affecting overall well-being and daily life. Navigating this emotional ride is no small feat, but understanding its impact is a crucial step toward finding balance.

- *Anxious behavior:* This involves actions or reactions fueled by feelings of unease, worry, or nervousness, often in anticipation of the unknown. Picture it as restlessness, excessive worrying, or steering clear of certain situations.

Identifying a negative behavioral cycle is the first step toward change, and taking the right actions is crucial. Start with hope but strike a balance between realistic optimism and acknowledgment of limitations.

Hope is a powerful tool for navigating adversity, yet unchecked optimism can lead to misguided decisions. Misguided hope may cause individuals to overlook important issues, resulting in poor planning and jeopardized goals. It's important to remember that positive change is possible. The key lies in making wise decisions, focusing on good habits, and nurturing healthy relationships.

While hope is essential, it cannot be the sole strategy. True regeneration requires consistent effort, like growing a garden in ashes. It necessitates a conscious decision to nourish the inner self and initiate the process of mental and spiritual rejuvenation. Just as ash can provide fertile ground for growth, one must till their inner soil, feed it with nutrients, and plant the right seeds to experience rebirth and growth.

This is not a quick fix, but a gradual process of consistent, healthy practices that nourish the soul. Such transformation extends beyond recovering from a state of despair; it is a deep shift in perspective, a journey toward aligning the inner self with physical and mental well-being.

The path to recovery is long and arduous, requiring a commitment to overall wellness and challenging the quick-fix mindset prevalent in our society. Recognizing you are on the precipice of a breakdown emphasizes the urgency for action. Unfortunately, it is only when we are on the brink of collapse that the necessity for change becomes clear.

The key lies in early intervention, self-awareness, recognizing the signs, and taking proactive steps to mitigate the spread of negativity. It is time to depart from the land of the burnt and embrace a new path toward growth and fulfilment. As I once heard someone say, "You are not required to set yourself on fire to keep other people warm."

Take a minute to assess if you are living in the land of the burnt. The next exercise will help you evaluate your stress levels. It will help you pinpoint whether you are in a healthy space, on the road to burnout, or already in a state of ashes.

Stress can be insidious. We all have different stress thresholds, and our boundaries are easily crossed. In addition to emotional and psychological effects, the health consequences of unattended stress include autoimmune disease, inflammation, and coronary heart disease.

To avoid stepping over the line from stress to illness, it is important to have tools that help with balanced living.

Stress is a psychological process resulting from demands on an individual's coping resources. It can arise from a community, such as a workplace, family, or school, or external factors, such as financial stress, boredom, or poor physical health. Each person's triggers will be different. This is why it's crucial to know what stress looks and feel like to you. It is a highly personal experience unique to each individual. Understanding what triggers stress is empowering, enhancing self-awareness and enabling better self-care practices.

Pause, observe, and listen.

What Is Your Level of Stress?

Take a moment to evaluate if you are experiencing symptoms of burnout. The following questions can help you assess your stress levels, indicating whether you are in a healthy state, teetering on the edge of burnout, or already consumed by its effects.

Stress can manifest subtly, as everyone has a distinct threshold for managing it. Recognizing this limit can be difficult, leading to potential overexertion. Specific triggers or recurring events often induce stress. Identifying these triggers can guide you in recognizing when to pause, prioritize self-care, and rejuvenate.

A stress assessment comprehensively evaluates behaviors and encounters that provide valuable insights into your stress reactions. Invest time in thoughtfully and candidly responding to the following questions to better understand your individual stress patterns. Understanding triggers helps you grasp their impact better.

1. What makes you stressed?
2. What does stress look like to you?
3. What is your physical reaction to stress?
   - When I'm stressed, my mind tells me . . .
   - Stress makes my body feel like . . .
   - Stress makes me act like . . .

How do your responses to the above questions make you feel? Think about it.

Identifying your stress triggers is an essential first step toward effective stress management. Dive deep into your experiences, pinpoint the sources of your stress, and maintain a stress log to capture these triggers and your reactions to them. Embrace the power of self-care: prioritize time for activities that bring you joy or explore exciting new hobbies. A refreshing walk outdoors can work wonders. Nourish your body with nutritious meals, commit to regular exercise, and ensure you're getting enough sleep. Limit caffeine, practice mindfulness, and maintain perspective by being gentle with yourself. Assess requests against your priorities and steer clear of unhealthy coping mechanisms like smoking or excessive drinking.

You have the strength to transform your stress management journey—own it and let it empower you.

Most importantly, share your feelings with trusted individuals. If things become overwhelming, seek guidance from a doctor or mental health professional.

CHAPTER 2

Superwoman

From a young age, women are inundated with the belief that they can effortlessly juggle everything: work, family, and self-care, all at once. This pervasive image of a multitasking Superwoman has had a profound impact on women's careers and personal lives.

In the 1970s, viewers in the United States saw an Enjoli perfume ad that perfectly captured this "do everything" mindset. A woman in business attire sang that she was the ultimate multitasker—bringing home the bacon, frying it up, and making sure she attended to her man's needs. It was more than just an ad; it symbolized the feminist aspirations of the era. However, underlying this message was a paradoxical notion that women could effortlessly manage professional success, family responsibilities, and marital bliss.

Balancing a career, raising a family, and maintaining a personal life all at once is an immense challenge, made even more difficult by the unrealistic expectations that it can be achieved without meaningful support from others. Those who seem to manage it all likely outsource certain responsibilities, such as childcare, which can present its own set of challenges as children grow.

The Superwoman syndrome maybe be an unattainable expectation, but it has nevertheless become a societal norm—something we feel we should achieve. Many of us internalize this, striving for perfection only to stretch ourselves too thin.

It's time to reconsider our approach. Multitasking is not a badge of honor; it means operating at a fraction of our true potential. So why settle for less when we can prioritize and focus on what truly matters?

I consider myself an ambitious woman who has had a successful fifteen-year career in television journalism in the United States. However, everything changed when I became a mother at the age of thirty-six. Despite never envisioning myself as the maternal type, motherhood shifted my priorities in unexpected ways.

Adapting to this new role was a challenge, especially considering the societal expectations that I had internalized over the years. And then, our family made the move to Europe. While my British husband's career as a film producer flourished, I faced a period of uncertainty because of this major change.

Although I had promising opportunities in the UK, the unique challenges of my American accent, my skin color, and the nuances of British culture caught me off guard. I filmed two television series that never aired, which led me to question my next career steps.

This transition period forced me to reevaluate and reassess the direction of my life. I had to completely shift my perspective—and I did. My focus turned to raising our daughter and exploring new possibilities that this change could bring.

For the first time, I had to learn to slow down, a concept that felt foreign to me. As women, we are conditioned to keep pushing forward without seeking help, laboring under the illusion that we can handle everything. This experience made me realize that the idea of being a Superwoman is nothing more than a fictional character; we need to instead take care of the real person we actually are.

Regaining Our Balance

The relentless pressure to excel in every aspect of our lives, whether it's as mothers, professionals, wives, or homemakers, often takes a toll on our well-being. It manifests itself in various ways: anxiety, irritability, sleep disturbances, muscle tension, and more. We might dismiss these symptoms as mere consequences of a busy life, but in reality, they are signs of an imbalanced existence.

I recall a poignant moment when my sister visited me from New York. I was struggling to adapt and find my place in the UK, feeling overwhelmed and disappointed in myself. Seeking solace, I found myself crying alone in the bathroom, hidden from prying eyes. It was during this vulnerable moment that I realized I had been prioritizing everyone else's needs and expectations above my own. Incidentally, my sister found it absurd that I refused to reveal my vulnerability, particularly to her. Naturally, she would have been by my side, offering unwavering support in any way she could.

As women, we often find it challenging to prioritize ourselves, but neglecting our well-being is a disservice not only to ourselves but also to those around us. By disregarding self-care, we are ultimately failing not just ourselves, but also those we love and hold dear—those who count on us.

It is imperative that we dismantle the unrealistic societal framework that demands perfection and recognize the importance of pursuing balance. Prioritizing our well-being is not a sign of weakness but rather a testament to our self-awareness. Taking the necessary time for self-care allows us to thrive and grow.

Superwoman

Our bodies are wise messengers, rarely leading us astray. When we experience excessive sweating, difficulty concentrating, or the hollow feeling of apathy, it is our body's way of signaling that something is amiss. These physical and mental imbalances are reminders to tune in more deeply to our well-being. Unfortunately, our connection to our bodies and minds often gets disrupted amid the constant distractions of technology and the noise of the world around us.

This disconnection prevents us from truly hearing what our bodies are trying to communicate. Ignoring these signals inevitably leads to unpleasant consequences. Physical ailments, emotional exhaustion, and a decline in work performance may ensue. Yet we often dismiss these persistent issues as merely bad days while failing to recognize their significance.

As these negative symptoms persist, they begin to deeply affect us. We become accustomed to their presence, sometimes needing a major wake-up call, such as a health scare or a mental breakdown, to realize our limitations. It may feel isolating to confront this truth. But rest assured, you are not alone; many other people are navigating similar challenges.

Furthermore, "world sickness," the collective weight of unsettling societal chaos, the lack of strong leadership, and the relentless stream of negative news—exacerbates these struggles. It is crucial that we acknowledge and then address these factors as we strive for a healthier, more balanced existence. We need to tune out and tune in.

Let us prioritize our well-being and listen to the messages our bodies are sending. By doing so, we can reclaim our strength, resilience, and inner harmony. Together, we can challenge the norms, redefine success, and create a world where balance and self-care are valued.

Starting the day with something lighthearted, such as watching a silly video, can bring much-needed laughter. Or read something thoughtful like Ryan Holiday's book *The Daily Stoic*, which serves as a reminder that not everything is gloomy.

It's important to avoid pushing ourselves beyond human limitations and instead embrace our genuine emotions. Neglecting this aspect builds a wall of resistance around us, leading to isolation and a mindset of, "I can handle this; I don't need to feel." While this attitude may appear protective, it actually distances us from our true selves and our authentic emotions.

Internalizing Superwoman

As we've discussed, the archetype of Superwoman embodies an unattainable ideal of perfection. It portrays her as the ultimate achiever, effortlessly balancing all aspects of life without vulnerability. However, this concept, likely conceived by a man, sets an impossible standard for women. It promotes the idea of being flawless, always ready and capable, and easily outperforming others.

But let's face it, Superwoman is a cartoon character. She doesn't exist. No one can embody such perfection. Being labeled as Superwoman is not a compliment; it endorses an unsustainable myth.

I must admit that I once subscribed to this notion in my youth. As I grew older and took on more responsibilities, the Superwoman label became burdensome. The pressure is not always explicit; it often manifests subtly, making it even more challenging for us to face up to and address.

The COVID-19 pandemic further exposed how women bear the brunt of shared responsibilities. Working mothers suddenly found themselves confined to their homes, juggling professional duties with homeschooling their children while still managing the household. Despite the progressive gender roles most of us have come to adopt and adapt to, the default expectation during those months of lockdown sent us backward. The idea of men and women sharing responsibilities for home and family flew out the window, and many families reverted to traditional roles. Women were tasked with doing it all—holding down a job, caring for the children, running the home, carrying the emotional burden of that stressful time, and juggling anything else that came up.

Why did we go backward like that? Perhaps guilt played a role, as women—for years having internalized the myth that they could and should do it all—felt pressured to fulfill the impossible standard of the Superwoman syndrome.

In the midst of the global pandemic, my family's experience mirrored a larger social narrative. My home became both a sanctuary and a battleground, shared with my twenty-six-year-old daughter, my husband, and beloved dog. My husband, struggling to adapt, unintentionally shifted the emotional load onto my daughter and me.

This scenario is familiar in many households, where crises reveal underlying dynamics and the cracks become strained.

Amid it all, I juggled cooking, cleaning, and professional commitments. On Fridays, I hosted live sessions to support other women in AllBright, an international women's organization dedicated to building female leaders, going through similar challenges. I simply carried on because that's what we do. We persevere.

My experience in a newsroom proved invaluable during COVID-19. I thrive under pressure, which can be both advantageous and challenging. My husband has always been actively involved at home, a hands-on father since our daughter's birth and eager to help. However, I often kept him out of the kitchen and household chores because of my outdated belief that if you want something done right, you do it yourself. So three months into the pandemic, with my husband becoming increasingly stressed, I found myself juggling the roles of mother, wife, therapist, cook, cleaner, and breadwinner. To be fair, my husband successfully produced four feature films by the time the COVID-19 crisis ended. This was excellent for our finances, but the pressure involved in filmmaking took a toll on our household's well-being.

These interactions highlighted the pervasive reality that women often find themselves shouldering the dual burdens of home and work. This period was not just about survival; it was about adaptation and finding strength in the rhythms of domestic life while pursuing professional careers.

The challenge lies not only in fulfilling these roles but also in the internalization of this archetype. It ingrains in us the belief that personal sacrifice is synonymous with success, urging us to prioritize everything but ourselves.

However, the pressures of the pandemic also revealed the importance of self-care. We can't wait for someone else to care for us; we have to do this ourselves. Prioritizing our mental, physical, and emotional well-being is essential. It empowers us to be more present and effective in every aspect of our lives.

Sure, Superwoman may be lauded for her ability to prioritize others over herself, persevere through adversity, and maintain harmony. But let's not forget the invisible toll this role takes. It's time for a shift in how we value ourselves. And also to support the other women in our lives.

The Superwoman character embodies an impenetrable force field, a shield that repels pain, emotion, and personal struggles. This metaphorical armor symbolizes the sacrifice of one's own needs for the perceived greater good, leading to a dangerous disconnection from one's voice.

Such a perspective is fundamentally flawed. And as the next story reveals, it won't repel what may be your biggest enemy—*you*.

Sophie's Story

Meet my client Sophie, an extraordinary individual driven by an unwavering pursuit of success. Originally from Australia, Sophie has set her sights on achieving significant wealth and prosperity abroad. In her thirties, Sophie possesses a remarkable combination of intelligence, charm, and ambition that sets her apart. Nothing can deter her. However, this relentless pursuit eventually became an obstacle in her own path.

In her earlier years, Sophie sought to fill the void of an unhappy family dynamic by adopting a people-pleasing persona. She prioritized the needs of others above her own, striving to secure the happiness of everyone in her orbit. This

Superwoman

characteristic endured into adulthood, shaping her interactions with the world.

Fueled by ambition, she secured admission to the world-famous Harvard Business School. Upon graduation, she embarked on a transformative journey, starting at a renowned finance firm, then venturing into the startup world, and ultimately attaining a VP position at a cutting-edge tech company. Despite her remarkable achievements, Sophie felt unappreciated for her tireless efforts. This spurred her to strive even harder for the recognition she felt she deserved. Regrettably, Sophie's unwavering dedication to her career led her straight into the flames.

"I think a lot of the time, you don't realize what's happening until it's too late. So you asked me what does burnout look like? Well, I was blind to it. And that's the issue. That's why so many women find themselves in that situation. Because we're smart. And if we knew what was happening, in theory, we would do something about it."[6]

Sophie made the bold decision to uproot her life and move to London, entrusted with the task of establishing a European branch for her tech company. This meant living in London while working on New York time. She relentlessly pursued the senior VP position, which resulted in a whirlwind of transatlantic

---

6   Sophie, interview by the author, October 1, 2023, New York City. All other quotations from Sophie in this chapter come from this interview.

flights—and neglecting her personal life and well-being in the process.

"I was exhausted. But there's some sort of drive that exists inside you. That keeps you pushing, pushing to show that you can continue to deliver, that you're strong, that you're not a weak person. You can keep up with the best of them. And it's almost the more tired you get, the more fear you have of being found out for not being able to hack it, so it spirals."

She believed she could handle it all, conforming to the Superwoman model. However, the toll it took on her was immense. As she continued at this frantic pace, a sense of resentment toward her job began to creep in. Yet the drive for success acted as an irresistible force.

Her boss, a master manipulator of emotions, created an illusion of a personal connection, making her feel indispensable. And so she soldiered on, donning her cape and turning a blind eye to the impending burnout.

"I care what other people think too much. I didn't want to let anyone down. But in doing that, I let myself down. But again, I was so deep in that hole that I couldn't see that. It's as though the need to check off items on the to-do list just goes out of control . . . but you're desperate to, and you almost do anything to get to the top of that pile. It's as though you're trying to climb Everest every day."

Superwoman

Amid all of this, she was also grappling with the idea of starting a family. Her biological clock was ticking, yet she felt torn between prioritizing her career and personal life. It was becoming evident that she needed to put herself first.

Gradually, she reached a breaking point because of overwhelming fatigue. It was at this moment that her self-preservation instincts took over. She paused, reevaluated, and discovered the immense power of uttering a single, beautiful word: no.

Sophie embarked on a journey to establish firm boundaries, resolutely refusing to let others infringe on them. Inspired by her boyfriend, whose drive may not have matched hers but who embodied a more harmonious way of life, she began envisioning a life that was both distinct and brimming with success.

Making herself a priority, she cherished her own needs and desires. And when she finally summoned the courage to use that powerful word, "no," her worth in the eyes of her superiors soared to new heights. Sophie's line manager, the CEO, always saw her immense value to the organization. That's why he often dangled the allure of promotions and raises before her. Knowing Sophie struggled with self-doubt, he cleverly counted on her to keep saying "yes" to tasks she should have turned down.

As soon as she announced her pregnancy, they provided support. This is a classic example of a situation where one is taken advantage of until one recognizes one's own worth. After nearly reaching a point of total burnout, Sophie finally recognized her value.

Now, with her partner and young son, she experiences greater happiness, balance, and a deep appreciation for her worth. She fully embraces what she brings to the table, and her actions speak louder than words.

The Pitfalls of Self-Deception

This narrative is all too familiar, isn't it? That inner voice pleading for a break is often present, but we become experts at tuning it out, consumed by our commitments and ambitions.

Many of the clients I have worked with promise themselves they'll step back "soon," but they seldom do. And when they do step back, it's often too late—and only comes about after they reach rock bottom.

This pattern, where ambition and the desire to please trample over our basic needs, is something I have witnessed time and time again among the clients I coach. Despite my advice, it remains a trap that many fall into. I have personally experienced it, knowing exactly what my clients are thinking and providing advice they are reluctant to take.

It's the trap of our internal wiring.

We must acknowledge this pitfall and recognize the importance of rewriting this Superwoman narrative. We must learn to value self-care as much as we value ambition.

Entering the world as a "princess of power" is an exercise in self-deception. You assume the role perfectly, but beneath the surface, you're disengaged, more of a shell than a presence. This disconnect stems from a lack of genuine focus and vitality. Outwardly you may look complete, yet inwardly you're running on empty.

In this role, you ignore your deeper instincts, mechanically going through the motions. You've convinced yourself of your full participation and effectiveness, but it rings hollow—you don't really believe it. This self-deception betrays your true capabilities as you cling to a false narrative of empowerment, repeating the mantra, "I have the power." But the hard reality is that such power is a myth, at odds with our human nature and particularly misaligned with the female experience. Embracing this illusion sets us up for inevitable exhaustion and disillusionment.

The Shitkicker Mentality

Here's another term: shitkicker. It refers to someone who gets things done, pushing aside obstacles with determination and strength. However, this "shitkicker" mentality often involves a relentless pursuit without pausing to reflect on the significance of challenges. It is not about mindful action, but rather about barreling forward without truly understanding the lessons those challenges hold. This approach lacks connection and understanding, driven solely by an undefined goal.

We tend to adopt this mindset because we believe we should plow through anything that stands in our way. But what do we truly gain from all this relentless pushing? In this pursuit, what deeper connections and meaningful experiences are we sacrificing? What valuable insights are lost in the constant motion and noise?

The practice of active listening is abandoned in this rush. When life becomes a series of obstacles, it becomes difficult to distinguish between friend and foe, opportunity and distraction. The relentless pursuit of a destination becomes detached from its value and impact. The broader context is ignored, and our focus narrows to immediate challenges, obscuring larger objectives and potential alliances. Instead of clearing the path, we become too engrossed in small battles, oblivious to the ongoing war. We forget the big picture—what we're really fighting for.

Adopting the persona of Superwoman and relying solely on self-sufficiency leads us down a destructive path. It may make us appear formidable, but that comes at a significant cost. This approach alienates others, creating an environment of intimidation rather than collaboration and support.

Leaders who ascend through fear may reach the top, but they'll find themselves at a lonely peak, drained emotionally and isolated. Despite its initial appeal, this path leads to profound disconnection from oneself and others.

The myth of Superwoman portrays an image of invincibility as if she were forged from titanium. Strong. Untouchable. Invulnerable. However, this mindset is dangerously deceptive, fostering the belief that one is impervious to harm or failure. Despite clear signs of wear and tear (both physically and mentally), there is a clinging to the illusion of being an exception.

I have personally traveled down this treacherous road, convinced of my immunity to the consequences of relentless stress and overexertion. I used to think, "That won't happen to me." But reality has a way of catching up to us.

In my case, it was my back that gave way, resulting in the need for a literal restructuring, complete with a metal cage and screws. Ignoring the advice of doctors years earlier and foolishly believing I was above the physical demands I placed on myself led me directly to that operating table.

This is not solely about neglecting physical health; it encompasses a mindset of denial, falsely believing in an impenetrable armor that shields us from the inevitable. But here's the sobering truth: No one is exempt. Trusting in one's exceptionality is a misguided sense of security. Wrapped in this illusionary cover, we ignore the very real vulnerabilities we all face. It sets us up for a rude awakening when reality finally comes crashing down.

Disregarding the signs and embracing a sense of invincibility is sheer folly. It paves a direct path to unforeseen and often harsh consequences. Let us instead acknowledge our limitations and treat ourselves with the care and respect we deserve.

Goddess of Love and War

Imagine Superwoman, a fusion of Aphrodite and Athena, embodying both love and war. She embodies Athena's unwavering spirit, the epitome of a strong woman, intertwined with Aphrodite's nurturing heart. Yet her power transcends mere physical strength; it encompasses emotional intelligence and resilience, a harmonious blend of the emotional and the physical.

From my personal experience, I know that Black women often carry the perception of possessing an extraordinary level of resilience. It's as if we have an innate additional layer of fortitude. This perception finds its roots in historical traumas such as slavery, where we endured unimaginable hardships, faced separation from family, and endured the heart-wrenching loss of our children. And yet we are still expected to toil tirelessly and care for our families.

However, this stereotype, coupled with the expectation of inherent strength and endurance, becomes a burdensome weight to bear. It significantly affects Black women, who confront a multitude of systemic challenges that are often overlooked or taken for granted.

These challenges manifest in the form of daily microaggressions, subtle insults, being taken for granted, or the burden of being the sole representative of Black women at decision-making tables. These experiences are not limited to external struggles; they shape our identity and influence our interactions with the world.

During the pandemic, many Black women had the opportunity to work from the comfort of their homes. This newfound perspective brought forth a revelation. Liberated from the need to maintain a "professional" facade, many hesitated to return to the traditional office setting.

Why? Because of their desire to break free from code switching—the constant preoccupation with appearances, whether it be hair, speech, food, or the exhaustion of perpetually wearing our metaphorical armor to fit in.

This reality exposes the falsehoods of the Superwoman stereotype that society has imposed on us and which we, in turn, have internalized. The notion of invincibility, the expectation to shoulder endless burdens, is a deception.

I unequivocally reject this notion of Superwoman. I focus on prioritizing my well-being and caring for those I love, and I can only achieve this by putting myself first.

Shed the Guilt

When it comes to the contrast between love and war, it is indeed true that women possess inherent fierceness and protectiveness, especially when it concerns our own. Our emotional intelligence often manifests as empathy and caregiving.

However, the notion of embodying a goddess of both love and war, juggling these immense responsibilities, is a fallacy. Trying to be the protector, career manager, and emotional support for others all at once is simply unsustainable. Yet we often feel a deep-rooted sense of duty and empathy, which leads to guilt when we fall short of these self-imposed expectations. This inclination to prioritize others over ourselves comes at the expense of our well-being and our ability to not only survive but thrive.

This pattern is partly a result of societal conditioning and partly self-inflicted. We must free ourselves from this unnecessary guilt. Prioritizing self-care is not selfish; it is vital for preserving our capacity to genuinely care for others. When we are off balance, truly caring for others becomes an impossibility.

The Superwoman syndrome is akin to being tethered to an endless list of tasks, constantly burdened by the pressure to complete them all. It is a cycle that leaves us asking, "How can I possibly tackle all of this?" and subsequently drowning in guilt when we inevitably fall short.

The struggle of working through this list, crossing off items but never reaching the end, breeds a mix of frustration, depression, and overwhelming exhaustion.

So here's my advice: Drop the cape!

That Superwoman cape is not your salvation; it is an anchor that drags you down. It is time to release that weight and liberate yourself.

Beneath that cape lies your true strength, your ability to rise and soar on your own terms, unburdened by the impossible demands you have placed on yourself and those imposed by others.

Living in alignment with our personal values requires discernment and awareness of what truly matters. By understanding our values, we can lighten the burden of insignificant matters and prioritize what holds the utmost importance. This empowers us to choose where we invest our care, while reducing the significance of others' opinions and desires.

As philosopher and author Eric Hoffer once said, "A man is likely to mind his own business when it is worth minding. When it is not, he takes his mind off his own meaningless affairs by minding other people's business."[7]

How's Your Self-Care?

Caring about the right things involves prioritizing what truly matters, making deliberate choices aligned with our values, and taking effective action. By eliminating what doesn't matter and focusing on what is important, we can avoid wasting time and energy on unimportant things. This can lead to a sense of fulfilment and reduce negative emotions like stress and anxiety.

I urge you to delve deep into the following activities to discover where you stand on self-care.

Know what is genuinely important to you. We often invest excessive time and energy into matters that hold little significance in our lives. Women, in particular, tend to prioritize the needs of others over their own. Take a moment to reflect. Are you living in harmony with your values, beliefs, purpose, and passions? It might be time to assess how you allocate your energy and then make the necessary adjustments. Reevaluate your focus to align with your life's priorities, shedding light on

---

[7] Eric Hoffer, *The True Believer* (Harper and Row, 1951), section 10.

what truly matters while releasing anything trivial that drains your energy.

Create a list of your values and clarify their significance. Understanding your values and beliefs is vital for crafting a path toward happiness and success. Identifying your core values allows you to concentrate on what truly matters to you, be it family, friends, achievement, wisdom, kindness, or equity. Amid life's rapid pace, we often lose touch with these values, leading to uncertainty. Revisiting your values will realign you with life's essence. Embrace values that anchor you and embody your integrity—even if they don't conform to societal standards.

Considering your values, introspect. Answer these questions:

- How have you been investing your time and resources?
- What occupies your mind lately?
- Do you have any sources of stress?
- Where do you find value and love?
- Reflect on what brings you joy or discontent.
- Identify what you couldn't control but held on to.
- Who or what drains your energy?

Evaluate whether your actions align with your values, beliefs, and passions. Assess how you allocate your energy—is it in line with what matters to you? Prioritize your needs by letting go of behaviors that don't enhance your life. Break free from detrimental habits that hinder your growth. Opt for self-appreciation as your norm for personal development. Serving yourself well enables you to serve others effectively.

CHAPTER 3

Where There's Smoke, There's Danger

When ignited, burning sage begins with tiny sparks, eventually producing smoldering embers and wisps of smoke. This slow and methodical burning process reminds me of the gradual evolution of gender dynamics and the journey toward women's empowerment.

Change in this environment does not happen overnight. Gender equality is built on small, persistent efforts. Instances where women's voices are stifled, their achievements are overshadowed, or when they are relegated to secondary roles are like the sparks. Though seemingly minor, these sparks can potentially ignite significant change through collective action.

For example, in the workplace, women are often pigeonholed into housekeeping roles like event or party planning, while men are assigned more high-profile tasks. It is as if women are expected to keep everything running smoothly in the background, while men take the helm and bask in the spotlight.

Such a bias toward placing men in high-stakes roles can fuel a slow-burning resentment among women. And this simmering resentment is like a curl of smoke, signaling impending change. It's a nagging sensation that something is amiss, even if you can't quite pinpoint it. These experiences, though seemingly small, accumulate over time, eroding your confidence and self-worth.

As this resentment grows, you may start to feel its burn. Often, the source of this discomfort is not immediately obvious. It's not always about blatant sexism or lack of male support, although these certainly play a role. Rather, it's a culmination of various factors that feed a growing fire, eventually producing enough smoke to signal danger.

Blinded by the Smoke

Reaching this point means becoming accustomed to the burn of these issues, not realizing that you are amid smoke, slowly being consumed. You continue as usual, oblivious to the emotional, mental, and physical toll. Yet becoming desensitized to a situation makes it harder to recognize its impact.

As the pandemic unfolded, women faced an unprecedented reality check, facing the absurdity of juggling work, household duties, childcare, and maintaining an immaculate home. This Herculean effort quickly led to overwhelming burnout.

Even the most industrious women began to question the feasibility of "doing it all" and the value of their exhaustive endeavors. They found themselves engulfed in metaphorical smoke, suffocating from their relentless exertion.

This smoke not only drains your energy but also cloaks your aspirations, erodes your individuality, and saps your drive. Life becomes a dense fog, obscuring clarity and leaving you feeling lost and despondent. You've become blinded by the smoke that is the start of burnout.

If you do notice that smoke, you might ask yourself, "How long have I been burning out?"

Yet we have learned to function on the brink of collapse. It is evident in our scattered thoughts, faltering memory, and that persistent question, "What is wrong with me?" We promise ourselves change but struggle to break free from this deeply ingrained pattern, pushing ourselves to the point of breaking.

Many women are trapped in this cycle, continuing until they hit a wall. There is a fear of what stopping might reveal, a strange comfort in the familiar pain of constant burnout. The prospect of pausing to reassess brings anxiety and fears of facing potentially greater challenges, leading many to cling to their punishing routines.

What is crucial to understand is the inevitability of burnout in such a smoky environment. It is like staying in a smoke-filled room, detrimental to your well-being and requiring immediate action to prevent irreversible damage.

Neglecting your feelings and disregarding the concerns of those around you is a direct path to burnout. Think of it as recovering from severe burns. While not a physical injury, it represents a profound erosion of your emotional, mental, and physical health, corroding your essence and necessitating significant self-care for recovery.

In this process, questions like, "Why did I let this happen?," "How did I get here?," and "Where did I go wrong?" often arise, accompanied by guilt. While personal accountability plays a role—yes, you made some bad decisions—much of this burden stems from broader systemic societal pressures and expectations.

Think of the analogy of being splattered by hot grease while cooking. It inflicts a sharp, immediate pain that fades with first aid but leaves a mark. The physical pain of burnout may subside, but the scar will remain.

White Male Entitlement

In our society, there exists a deeply ingrained belief that reinforces the idea of inherent entitlement for White men to lead, succeed, and hold power, solely based on their race and gender. This sense of entitlement has deep historical roots and is perpetuated by a specific narrative that has often championed the notion of White supremacy.

Throughout history, women were marginalized and treated as property, only gaining recognition as individuals in more recent times. African Americans have endured a long history of oppression and discrimination. Even today, we can observe the stark presence of White male entitlement in society's power structures, often embodied by older generations who cling to outdated norms that equate their identity with inherent authority and wealth.

It is important to acknowledge and address this issue, as it undermines the principles of equality and justice that we strive for in a society underpinned by caste.

This privilege often plays out in the educational and professional environments, where family ties trump merit, allowing individuals with influential names to gain unearned advantages, such as admission to elite institutions or coveted positions, irrespective of their true capabilities.

Nepotism and legacy preservation continue to uphold privilege, resulting in a perception that even the most disadvantaged White men are more competent than Black women, who find themselves at the bottom of the social hierarchy by birth. This perpetuates a false narrative of superiority, which demoralizes all women and instills doubt about their abilities and the fairness of the system.

While women are hired for their achievements, men are hired for their perceived potential.

Injustice breeds a sense of futility, leaving us feeling locked out from opportunities that seem only theoretically accessible. This situation is further exacerbated by societal conditioning and a lack of substantial challenge to the status quo.

What can we do to change this? We must start by acknowledging our own complicity in perpetuating these systems. By failing to actively challenge these norms, we inadvertently contribute to their persistence.

True change demands more than passive acknowledgment. It necessitates active and forceful opposition to break the cycle of privilege and open doors for genuine merit and equality—regardless of race, gender, or class (caste).

Of course, the vicious cycle will persist as long as too many of us remain passive observers.

Lacking Access to Power

Access to power remains a significant hurdle for many women and people of color in professional environments.

As we strive for influential positions, the path is often fraught with unexpected and additional challenges. Even when we secure a seat at the table, we quickly discover the unique obstacles of being in the minority, feeling like we are set up to fail.

After my client's global marketing agency lost three major accounts, the predominantly male board made an interesting choice. They appointed the only woman, a lawyer with no advertising or marketing background, to head the company. Such decisions often appear destined for failure. Then, they thought placing a woman in a top position would create an illusion of addressing the issue. However, if she failed, the blame would rest solely on her shoulders.

Imagine if the board had instead set up a subcommittee dedicated to tackling client concerns, led by its newly appointed female chair and filled with a diverse mix of stakeholders from across the agency. This team could have brought fresh perspectives on what clients really want and what consumers need. By involving stakeholders, it would have given them a voice, shared the responsibility of updating the company's values, and helped propel the agency into the twenty-first century. Now, that would have been a win-win situation.

It was the structural barrier of the "old boys' network" and that homogenous perspective that was increasingly causing my client's ad agency to lose longstanding accounts. The perception of an entrenched network favoring men became an unattractive proposition. Realizing a fundamental culture change was necessary for continued success, a Black woman was appointed to the board, in addition to the female who was appointed CEO. This move brought more diverse perspectives into the decision-making process.

By having more than one minority voice, the new female CEO could help drive meaningful change.

The task of challenging deep-seated cultural norms and systemic barriers can be daunting, especially when someone tries to do this on their own. Acting alone, minorities are often overlooked or unfairly labeled as troublemakers and are burdened by the pressure to conform, leading to a forced silence.

Being the sole voice in the room has been a personal challenge, often leaving me as the lone unicorn at the table. While this position allows me to offer a unique perspective, it can be tough to make my voice heard. I once served on a board alongside some of the biggest names in the film industry, individuals with liberal views and good intentions, who aimed to start a school to recruit and train underrepresented groups for film careers—a truly commendable mission. They saw the value in having me involved, yet consistently missed chances to build a leadership structure that mirrored the communities they hoped to serve. As I pointed this out time and again, their frustration was palpable.

After George Floyd's tragic murder in Minneapolis in May 2020, I was asked to take the helm of the DEI subcommittee. With passion and a treasure trove of proven strategies, I accepted the challenge to propel our school toward its diversity goals. Yet despite escalating incidents of racial abuse and dwindling morale among our ethnic staff, my recommendations faded into obscurity.

Even with well-meaning colleagues, sidelining an expert with lived experience and a solid track record in driving cultural change is a wake-up call. It's a signal to reassess your position and avoid simply being a figurehead at the table. Still, this experience won't deter me from joining more boards and making sure my voice is heard. It's all about knowing when to step back, but never giving up on making an impact.

Women often feel this lack of access to power, even if they are competent and skilled, as their contributions are consistently unnoticed or attributed to others. It is like being relegated to task-oriented roles while high-profile projects go elsewhere (to a male colleague's desk), a practice often accepted without question.

I have raised this observation with various leaders, who typically respond with, "They [the men] are just better at it," which is a rather unfortunately pervasive form of sexism.

Women now need to proactively confront these issues to prevent them from becoming normalized. The absence of women in leadership roles, such as CEOs or board members, reinforces the notion that such positions are unattainable for us.

The old aphorism holds true in these situations of being underrepresented: "You cannot be what you cannot see." We need more role models who demonstrate that power positions are accessible to each of us, regardless of our background.

The spark that ignites change often feels like another grease burn. We are startled when someone deserving is overlooked for a position, prompting questions like, "Why weren't they considered?"

I often hear women say, "I never asked for that board seat," revealing a critical part of the problem. It is a classic case of, "Don't ask, don't get." It's time to put *gimme* in your vocabulary.

Being Invisible

Feeling unnoticed and unappreciated at work can be incredibly painful, often resulting from seemingly insignificant incidents. Take, for example, when senior management repeatedly forgets your name despite your noteworthy contributions, or confuses you with another colleague who happens to be female or non-White (as I have personally experienced). These instances leave you with the disheartening impression that you are not seen as an individual, but rather reduced to the color of your skin.

It is also quite common to see women being assigned menial tasks, no matter their position or achievements. Regardless of their rank, women often find themselves being asked to fetch coffee or tea, being treated more as secretaries rather than equals. Imagine a male CEO turning to the new Ivy League male hire and saying, "I'll take my coffee with milk, no sugar."

This issue extends beyond hierarchical dynamics; it is pervasive and fueled by deeply ingrained cultural biases. There is often an automatic assumption that women, especially women of color, are in a supportive role rather than the ones making important decisions.

Constantly having to assert your authority and clarify your position, fighting against the presumption of powerlessness due to gender epitomizes the feeling of being invisible. This contributes to a metaphorical smokescreen that erodes self-esteem and weighs heavily on one's spirit. It is like being shrouded in fog, where your hard work and significant achievements go unnoticed, blending you into the faceless crowd who simply "get things done."

A significant part of this issue arises from our own behavior as women, specifically our hesitation in trumpeting our accomplishments and asserting our right to recognition openly. This skill does not come naturally to many of us.

Throughout history, societal expectations have dictated that women (like children) should be seen but not heard. The mindset of keeping your head down, working hard, and being rewarded still persists in today's business world. For instance, an extreme example is Afghanistan, where women are not only confined to the background, with their roles limited to domestic responsibilities, but are now forced to be completely covered and not allowed to make eye contact in public. They are expected to serve as mere adornments to men rather than as active participants in public or professional domains.

Despite progress in many areas, these deeply ingrained norms continue to exist even in modern societies, perpetuating the cycle of rendering women invisible in professional settings.

The Fix-It Ladies

The "fix-it lady" is a familiar archetype in the workplace. She's the go-to person for resolving issues, the one who lives by the motto "If you want it done right, do it yourself."

She often volunteers with a reassuring, "Leave it to me! I'll handle it!" However, her eagerness to shoulder extra burdens can unwittingly hinder her career progression. Being perpetually weighed down with additional tasks can obscure her potential for other roles or promotions. While she garners praise for her reliability and dedication, it doesn't always lead to professional advancement.

If you find yourself constantly in this "fix-it lady" role, it's crucial to know when to step back. Often, you might be informally taking over responsibilities that officially belong to someone else. The challenge is that excelling in such a role can become a comfort zone, making it hard to let go of that role.

Immersed in a demanding role, it's easy to lose self-awareness and a sense of direction. It usually takes an external perspective or a concerned individual to highlight the need for a change, as if clearing the smoke to reveal new possibilities. Gaining such an outside perspective can sharply bring into focus the need for you to change. An external viewpoint is important for identifying the right moment to act, like someone offering a fire extinguisher before it becomes a raging fire.

This external perspective often comes from a coach or mentor, rather than friends or family. They serve as impartial observers, providing a frank assessment of your situation.

Their advice might be surprising, direct, and unvarnished. They could suggest unexplained opportunities, question your commitment to a stagnating role, or encourage you to venture into new territories, reminding you of your worth.

While the thought of leaving a challenging situation or exploring a new career path can be daunting, it's often a step toward personal growth and fulfilment. Remember, change doesn't have to be a drastic, immediate leap. It's normal for transitions, like securing a new position, to take several months. The encouraging aspect is that once you start applying and putting yourself out there, your chances of finding new opportunities increase significantly.

But don't rush the process. Take it one step at a time, and you have a good chance of bringing about great change in your life.

Imbalance of Pay and Financial Power

Few people would disagree that the gender wage gap—where women earn roughly eighty-two cents for every dollar a man earns doing the same work—leads to an imbalance of financial power. Those who earn more have more power than those who earn less. This imbalance, which occurs even in so-called progressive countries, is deeply rooted in longstanding cultural norms and biases, and those biases tend to be ingrained in all of us from an early age.

Not only does society value women in the workplace less than their male counterparts, but men often have the advantage in financial literacy. Early on, boys are traditionally taught financial skills like money management, while girls often miss out on these lessons, thus setting them on a different financial trajectory from the start. This early educational gap lays the groundwork for later financial disparities.

Yet the persistence of the gender pay gap, despite laws being in place prohibiting pay discrimination, is baffling to me. I realize that there are procedures for work scaling and deciding compensation, but pay discrimination for the same employment is illegal.

American actor Jennifer Lawrence learned she was being paid less than her male counterparts—notably costar Bradley Cooper, after hackers broke into the files of her employer, Sony Pictures. She says of the discovery, "When the Sony hack happened, and I found out how much less I was being paid than the lucky people with dicks, I didn't get mad at Sony. I got mad at myself."[8]

Across the pond in the UK, consider the case of BBC broadcasters in 2018, where highly skilled female broadcasters discovered they were earning at least 9.3 percent less than their male counterparts.[9] These disparities not only create confusion

---

8 Helaine Olen, "Jennifer Lawrence and Bradley Cooper Have Us Wondering: Why Don't More People Discuss Their Compensation?" *Slate*, October 19, 2015, https://slate.com/human-interest/2015/10/jennifer-lawrence-bradley-cooper-and-compensation-why-aren-t-we-more-open-about-what-we-make.html.

9 "Timeline: How the BBC Gender Pay Story Has Unfolded," BBC, January 29, 2018, https://www.bbc.com/news/entertainment-arts-42833551.

but also leave women feeling undervalued and questioning their own worth.

Interestingly, executives in the C-suite know about these pay differences, and a handful of male executives have taken steps to address this issue by reducing their own salaries.[10] However, achieving systemic change in wealth distribution at the upper echelons remains a challenge.

A major obstacle lies in the cultural taboo of openly discussing money; it's often seen as gauche, tacky, or simply unacceptable. Nevertheless, if I were ever faced with being paid less than a counterpart for the same job, I would not hesitate to address it. In fact, I would even consider taking legal action if necessary. Talk money to me!

The exasperating gender pay gap serves as a stark reminder of our reluctance to openly discuss money, despite its direct correlation with power. Why do we shy away from addressing this critical issue?

It is inspiring to witness male allies who shoulder responsibility and make sacrifices to address these disparities. However, there remains a need to eliminate such inequalities at their core. This requires a collective effort to challenge the status quo and advocate for fair compensation for equal work.

While some may deem me a troublemaker, I embrace the

---

10   "Timeline: How the BBC Gender Pay Story Has Unfolded."

moniker, for silence only serves those in positions of power. As women, let us stand united, transcending society's fixation on appearances, and take decisive action. Our true strength lies in our collective endeavors.

Too Often Ignored

In today's world, it is disheartening to witness highly educated and hardworking women struggle to attain financial success, often striving merely to sustain a modest living with little left for savings. This predicament necessitates discipline, a virtue that is not always encouraged but is worthy of prioritization.

In fields like STEM and technology, where female representation is low, we see further evidence that women are not encouraged to approach things logically. But this is wrong-headed. Combining logic with empathy is crucial for our well-being.

I have personally experienced the sting of being ignored and feeling invisible. Being among the pioneering contributors to the Los Angeles bureau of the CNBC television network, I experienced a sense of indifference from the corporate headquarters on the East Coast. Not only was I undercompensated and undersupported, but it felt as if all of the stakeholders were treated as unwanted stepchildren within the network. Consequently, the office morale remained consistently low.

THE QUIET BURN

As we wrapped up our inaugural year as a budding network, the CEO flew into LA for a dinner with the bureau staff. We anticipated our bureau chief would seize the moment to champion our cause. Yet, true to his gentle and nonconfrontational nature, he remained silent. That moment, to be honest, ignited a fire within me. Summoning the courage, fortified by a few martinis, I took the bull by the horns and boldly told the CEO we were fed up with being undervalued, underserved, and underpaid. Judging by the stunned looks on everyone's faces when I finished, my speech must have had a few colorful words sprinkled in! Speaking up seemed imperative for self-preservation, notwithstanding the consequence of not renewing my contract. Victories may elude us at times, but my pursuit of justice remains unwavering.

The bottom line is that I felt driven to spotlight injustice. Sure, I might have needed a bit of liquid courage to kick things off, but ultimately, I wasn't afraid of losing my job by calling out a wrongdoer! I trusted that if one door closed, another would swing open—and it certainly did. In the aftermath, I felt empowered and liberated. I had spoken my truth, standing up not just for myself, but for all of us.

Life can sometimes feel like a dance with fire, where it becomes difficult to distinguish between smoke and actual flames. Not every situation offers an escape from the smoke, and sometimes we feel the pain of the burn too late.

What is important is having the courage to face these moments, to stand up for what is right, and to harness our power to light the way forward, even amid the flames.

Boundaries Exercise

Setting boundaries is essential because no one can respect limits they don't know exist. Some people will always push, talk, or demand beyond what's comfortable for you. Letting this happen repeatedly can take a toll, leading to low self-esteem, unmet needs, a lack of life control, and mounting stress, anxiety, and resentment. It can even hurt your work performance. So take charge and set those boundaries for a healthier, more balanced life! Scan the QR code in Figure 3.1 to learn more about the joys of being seen and heard.

In this empowering exercise, you'll craft an action plan for handling those who disregard your boundaries. The aim?

Figure 3.1. How it feels to be seen and heard by setting boundaries

Boost your self-awareness to spot rising stress in challenging moments before it overwhelms you. You'll also discover calming techniques that resonate with you, allowing you to respond thoughtfully rather than react impulsively.

- Consider moments when your boundaries have been compromised by individuals or situations. Make a detailed list of those interactions.
- Now think about how those compromises made you feel. Were you hurt, ashamed, embarrassed, angry? Be specific and write it down.
- Considering your responses to the above questions, how could you have better handled the situation for a more favorable outcome?
  - Take a breath and count to ten.
  - Remain silent and let your inner voice tell you to take the emotion out of the situation.
  - Leave the situation by walking away with the thought of self-preservation.

CHAPTER 4

From Imposter to Formidable Force

True power is not about merely surviving but about thriving. It lies in our ability to excel. For women, this means recognizing our inherent value and unleashing our boundless potential to reshape the world.

Moreover, it is crucial for us to tap into our collective strength. We must unite more often, for our combined power is formidable even though it's usually underestimated. Sure, we're making efforts to unify our efforts, but so far we're falling short of the scale necessary to dismantle deeply entrenched systems of authority and transform global dynamics.

Furthermore, progress is hindered by a pervasive lack of self-confidence among women in leadership. Their persistent doubts about their rightful place in positions of power have a domino effect and end up holding all of us back.

We have been conditioned to think small, but it is also a choice we make. As an executive leadership coach, I encounter incredibly talented women who are leaders in their respective fields, yet they doubt their rightful place at the table. When you delve deeper, you discover that they are uncertain about their own worth and purpose.

Imposter Syndrome

These high-achieving women are burdened by imposter syndrome, a creation I believe originated from men when we women began to seize opportunities and strive for success. This insidious syndrome relentlessly erodes the women's self-esteem. Often, I am overcome with frustration and an intense desire to jolt these capable clients out of this self-doubt.

When I witness this, I embody an external force, acting as a catalyst for change. Mine is a quest to delve into the depths of truth, peeling away layers to reveal the authentic, unadulterated core of each of these remarkable women. We are, each of us, amazing. Each of us has qualities that exemplify our abilities, and we must acknowledge them and wear them like a badge of honor.

We frequently shy away from the realities, even when confronted by irrefutable facts. We attribute our accomplishments to luck rather than merit, while some argue that we are merely tokens of diversity. Let this serve as a resounding call to action, a driving force to prove them wrong. Just as we aren't going to be held back by the myth of Superwoman, we won't be held down by the anchor of imposter syndrome.

Believing in your right to be where you are and striving for excellence are crucial. Actions always speak louder than words. What you truly need is inner strength, akin to a mother's instinct to protect her child, accessing that powerful, innate drive for self-preservation.

Force is about confronting the truth of becoming trapped in damaging mental and emotional cycles, often pushing you to the brink of burnout or a complete breakdown. We all experience that moment of realization when we notice a decline in our work performance, and we understand that something needs to change. Breaking these detrimental habits is imperative; otherwise, you're bound to crash and burn.

What Causes Imposter Syndrome?

Specific personality traits such as perfectionism, neuroticism, and inhibition have been associated with imposter syndrome.

Competitive environments can also evoke feelings of being an imposter. The experience of growing up under the weight of academic expectations or being in the limelight for accomplishments can trigger imposter syndrome. Moreover, feeling inadequate after facing failure in situations where success typically flows easily is common.[11]

If you're curious about whether you're harboring an imposter within, scan the QR code in Figure 4.1 to take this free test. You may surprise yourself.

According to the most recent KPMG Women's Leadership Summit Report, Imposter Syndrome affects a whopping 82 percent of the population, with 75 percent of women experiencing it in key moments in their current jobs or milestones in their careers.[12]

According to Valerie Young, PhD, there are five distinctive categories.

The Superwoman. The Superwoman is the epitome of dedication, putting in long hours and sacrificing personal time to excel in every aspect of life. Driven by the need to prove themselves as capable and accomplished, they seldom allow themselves a break.

---

11 "Imposter Syndrome," *Psychology Today*, accessed October 25, 2024, https://www.psychologytoday.com/gb/basics/imposter-syndrome.
12 KPMG, "Mind the Gap," December 2022, https://assets.kpmg.com/content/dam/kpmg/xx/pdf/2022/12/mind-the-gap.pdf.

From Imposter to Formidable Force

Figure 4.1. Imposter syndrome test

The Natural Genius. The Natural Genius is accustomed to effortlessly mastering tasks, making challenges or initial failures a blow to their self-image. Struggling with a concept can evoke feelings of shame and self-doubt, challenging their perception of innate ability.

The Soloist. The Soloist prefers independence and often hesitates to seek assistance. When they do reach out for help, they may battle feelings of incompetence or imposter syndrome, grappling with the discomfort of vulnerability.

The Expert. The Expert is dedicated to continuous learning, constantly pursuing additional certifications and training. Fueled by the belief that they must acquire extensive knowledge to be truly competent, they strive for perpetual growth and expertise in their field.[13]

If you identify with any of the above, I implore you to take a long, hard look at that imposter who is draining your energy and discover the real woman hiding behind that false face.

---

13   Valerie Young, *The Secret Thoughts of Successful Women* (Currency, 2011).

The following sections detail several things you can do to control your imposter syndrome.

Focus on the Facts

Imposter syndrome makes you feel like you aren't good at your job. But often, these feelings are based on fear—not reality. The best way to fight imposter syndrome is to separate feelings from facts. Emotions often override facts when you're under stress. Focus on your achievements and signature strengths instead.

Share Your Feelings

Imposter syndrome can create a sense of isolation. Avoid internalizing your feelings; recognize them so they can release their hold on you. Clinging to negative emotions can exacerbate this sensation. Opening up and discussing your thoughts with someone else can help. You might discover that your struggles are not uncommon, as imposter syndrome affects many individuals.

No One Is Perfect

You're only human. I'm not saying lower the bar, just adjust your standards for success. Stay focused on achieving your goal instead of being perfect. Come to an understanding of what is good enough. And if your expectations are not met, don't think of it as a failure; instead, reframe it as an opportunity to learn and grow.

Blow Your Own Horn

Do not hesitate to acknowledge your accomplishments. It's easy to become so focused on the results of our efforts that we overlook the importance of celebrating and sharing our successes. We may avoid sharing them with others out of fear of appearing boastful. However, it is crucial to acknowledge and take pride in your achievements. Please share them with others, let them inspire your future aspirations, and allow them to remind you of your capabilities and value.

Believe in yourself. Remember that you are capable and deserving of success. Don't let imposter syndrome stop you from reaching your full potential. Believe in your skills, knowledge, and experience.[14]

Take Care of Yourself

The imposter is not your friend. She's a bad companion. Let her go. If you can't banish her, keep her at arm's length and feed her facts, not emotions. You'll thank me later.

Taking care of yourself should be your top priority. Often, we tend to ignore the signs and hope that problems will resolve on their own. However, true strength comes from being disciplined

---

14 Ashley Abramson, "How to Overcome Imposter Phenomenon," *American Psychological Association* 52, no. 4 (2021), https://www.apa.org/monitor/2021/06/cover-impostor-phenomenon. See also Kess Eruteya, "You're Not an Imposter; You're Actually Pretty Amazing," *Harvard Business Review*, January 3, 2022, https://hbr.org/2022/01/youre-not-an-imposter-youre-actually-pretty-amazing.

and having the self-love to acknowledge your worth, while also being aware of your genuine needs.

Experiencing burnout goes beyond mere fatigue. It leaves you feeling empty and profoundly sad, and shaking off these feelings can be challenging.

Embrace Your Inner Strength

You are feeling so disconnected that you're struggling to recognize your own needs, let alone anyone else's. This is something you must confront head-on.

Discovering and embracing your inner strength is paramount. As the old saying goes, "When the going gets tough, the tough get going." You must persevere, diligently identifying early signs of burnout and effectively addressing them. This is the breakthrough you must manage to overcome these challenges.

Katherine's Story

My brilliant client Katherine, an angel investor, is currently recovering from mental exhaustion. She has undergone a transformation since divorcing an emotionally abusive man. This situation sheds light on the problem of misplaced priorities that have led to a constant state of emotional burnout.

Katherine had grown accustomed to a life of luxury, but it

came at a price. Raised in Europe, Katherine grew up in a family that placed great importance on material wealth. Consequently, she strived to amass her own fortune through high finance and eventually married a wealthy man. Yet, after saying "I do," she found herself making sacrifices.

She relinquished her dream job to relocate to another country for her husband, only to struggle to find a comparable opportunity for herself. When she became pregnant, she hired a nanny but wholeheartedly dedicated herself to raising her children. However, as time went on, she found herself not only managing the household and tending to her children's lives but also overseeing her husband's extracurriculars. She recalls:

> He was doing his thing, and I had his back. I had my kid's back and everyone's back. He was the provider when I was the manager. I organized him to go to watch the kids' football. He didn't do it. He chose whether he went or not, and he said to me, "The kids are not going to stop me from doing what I want." But it obviously stopped me from doing what I wanted. Nobody had my back. I was struggling with this, and I was also struggling with spending his money because I always had my own money, spending

THE QUIET BURN

> my money, earning my money, and then living very well with what I was earning. Then I wasn't, especially when I had the kids. I was still working, but not as much—part-time. I had to spend his money, and I really struggled with that.[15]

The weight of her responsibilities gradually eroded her self-esteem, sense of self-worth, and financial independence. She couldn't shake the feeling of being an imposter. Katherine began questioning her identity and wondered what had happened to the ambitious woman who'd once dreamed of building a fulfilling life for herself. In the midst of what should have been the best years of her life, Katherine found herself alone, lost in the fog of emotional burnout.

"I was reacting to life rather than proactively taking charge. Why did I not have my back? Having been a carer for my mother, I was on my own. And I was always on my own. I was and have been a lonely fighter. So that was what I did, and I didn't ask for help. And when I asked, I didn't get it because people didn't think I needed it. So I just soldiered on."

---

15   Katherine, interview by the author, October 10, 2023, United Kingdom. All quotations from Katherine in this chapter come from this interview.

Burnt to a Crisp

What happens when you come to the alarming realization that your life has veered off course, and you are not leading a fulfilling existence?

It's natural to feel a touch of melancholy, not the all-consuming kind, but enough to dampen your motivation. You find yourself neglecting the fundamentals, like skipping meals and neglecting exercise.

This gradual decline erodes your capacity to live a vibrant life. You start noticing warning signs of chronic stress, a loss of enthusiasm for life, and a disconnection from your work and the people around you.

For some, it takes a complete breakdown to realize that they have strayed from what truly matters—their values, passions, dreams, and purpose. They have become completely disconnected from their own needs, merely going through the motions.

Once self-help becomes unattainable, the essence of a fulfilling life becomes lost. You have become so detached from yourself that self-care feels foreign. Physically, mentally, and emotionally, you are drained. This is the breaking point, where someone needs to step in.

As Arianna Huffington once said, "The land of burnout is

not a place I ever want to go back to."[16] If you find yourself in this state of burnout, you need assistance. Others can see that you are unable to care for yourself.

I have experienced the suffocating grip of anxiety, recognizing its unmistakable signs: a racing heart, labored breath, an overwhelming loss of control, and sheer panic. Each encounter serves as a clear message to pause, recalibrate, and restore my equilibrium.

Thankfully, these episodes were neither long-term nor frequent, a testament to my keen awareness of when things start to go south. I pour myself into my work zealously, but I also know the value of stepping back, working out, nourishing myself, and refueling.

These invaluable lessons are deeply rooted in my experiences as an All-American swimmer. I'm an expert at keeping my head above water! Being a high-caliber athlete taught me the utmost significance of discipline, nutrition, self-respect, and an unwavering drive to achieve success. These principles are the bedrock of my character, blessing me with the resilience to overcome challenges while refusing to tolerate mistreatment.

As a Black woman, I was raised to reject the nonsense that

---

16   Arianna Huffington, "I Get 8 Hours of Sleep 95 Percent of the Time: Here's What Happens When I Don't," *Thrive Global*, May 18, 2018, https://thriveglobal.com/articles/i-get-8-hours-of-sleep-95-percent-of-the-time.

often comes my way, and I stick to that because I know it is part and parcel of my journey.

Not everyone gets these tools from the start. If you are missing them, you have got to either develop them or recognize the gap and forge those survival skills that reinforce your self-worth.

When you hit that point of being burnt to a crisp, surrender is your best bet. Let go, allow yourself to be nurtured, to experience life, and most importantly to cultivate self-love. That is where true strength lies.

Getting to the Truth

Self-love is not just a feel-good term. It is a formidable force, the kind of energy that fuels life itself. It is what keeps your inner flame alive.

Within each of us resides an inner voice of absolute truth, often obscured beneath layers of self-deception. We accumulate these layers, unwittingly muffling our voice until it can no longer break through with clarity.

Yet, when weariness sets in and passion wanes, these layers begin to dissolve, compelling us to confront the raw truth head-on. It is in these moments, when there is no longer any space for evasion, that the truth unveils itself boldly and inescapably right before our eyes.

We are experts at deceiving ourselves, spinning white lies that gradually darken into dangerous falsehoods. We say, "I'm fine," or "It's okay," or "Yes, I can do that." Self-deceit is saying these things when your inner voice screams the opposite. This leads to letting other people overstep your boundaries and treat you as if you're invisible.

All these contribute to feeling depleted and weary, eroding your ability to maintain those protective layers. Keeping up a facade is exhausting, and when your energy runs out, you are left facing the stark reality that something is drastically wrong.

But how do we get past this? Acknowledging that "I don't feel good" is a start.

When people say, "I don't feel like myself," it often means they are not treating themselves well, which ends up leading to physical, mental, or emotional distress, and sometimes even trauma. The moment of truth arrives when you have no choice but to face reality. When looking in the mirror becomes an undeniable confrontation with something amiss, that is when things shift. This realization becomes a catalyst for change and a force for good.

Truth, though sometimes painful, possesses the remarkable ability to inspire profound positive change and transformation. It also opens the possibility of turning that pain into something constructive. It is about choice, and how you respond and harness that truth.

From Imposter to Formidable Force

Liz's Story

Let me tell you about my old client and longtime friend Liz. This is a case of relentless burnout. Liz never aspired to become the director of production and acquisitions at a major film studio. However, when her husband passed away at a young age, she found herself raising their baby alone.

Driven by fear, she felt compelled to succeed in providing her daughter with the best life possible. Heavy responsibility had always been a familiar burden for Liz, starting from her early years as a little girl. Raised by a successful, single mother who led a vibrant life, she shouldered the weight of adulthood at a tender age.

Even today, putting herself last has become her default mode, a flame of perpetual burnout that has endured since time immemorial. Stress and anxiety are her constant companions. She describes it like this: "I think it's because I'm a single mother, and I was the daughter of a single mother. I was always the responsible one and the parent and kind of looking after my mom. But I also think, then being put in that position again with day-to-day, I was never able to put myself first."[17]

Liz's resilience is incredible, perhaps because she has had such a long time to build it. However, the consequence of that is

---

17   Liz, interview by the author, October 16, 2023, Los Angeles, California. All quotations from Liz in this chapter come from this interview.

she has also made little space in her life for nurturing herself in a way that is guided by self-worth. She lives in a pressure cooker.

"I think it has a physical toll on your body," she said. "I just generally feel tired, and then it's brain fog. I have days when I do probably four people's work. And I have days when I literally can't. Once I was working from home. I kept walking into rooms, and I had no idea why I'd walked into them. I broke a glass when I was trying to put it into the dishwasher. Someone asked me to do something, and it almost made me hysterical. I went on a call and said exactly the thing that I told myself I mustn't say, and then I turned my camera off and quietly wept."

A child with dubious parenting is often left with the feeling of being undeserving or not good enough. She counterbalances that insecurity by becoming the fix-it lady and Goddess of Love and War wrapped in one. Honestly, I don't know how Liz is still standing. It pains me to see any client managing this amount of stress daily. She's an enigma.

"It becomes very emotional, like a depression," she said. "It's like grief, and that grief is like the sea. One day it's really stormy. And the next day it feels really calm."

There is hope for Liz. Today she is more self-aware and realizes that being an eternal flame leads to nothing but ashes. She's discovered wild swimming to help her bring some balance into her life and to quell her habit of overspending to mask her feelings of inadequacy.

"The wild swimming and the cycling has really helped—the swimming particularly because I can't meditate in a traditional way. Actually, I'm not swimming for exercise. I'm actually outdoors in the cold looking at the sky, going, oh my God, it's beautiful to be alive."

Why Not Me?

We are often taught to keep our heads down, work diligently, and wait for recognition to come our way. However, this approach is fundamentally flawed. In the words of bell hooks, "If any female feels she needs anything beyond herself to legitimate and validate her existence, she is already giving away her power to be self-defining, her agency."[18]

If we don't take pride in our own accomplishments, if we fail to celebrate our achievements, we run the risk of fading into the background. Our successes may be overshadowed or even wrongfully claimed by others. This can trigger a destructive cycle of self-doubt, where we find ourselves repeatedly asking, "Why me?"

Instead, let's shift our focus to a more empowering question:

---

18 bell hooks, *Feminism Is for Everybody: Passionate Politics* (Routledge, 2015), 95.

"Why not me?" Let's recognize our own worth and insist on deserving success, recognition, and opportunities. By affirming our own values, we create a positive mindset that attracts the success we seek.

So let us raise our voices, share our achievements, and embrace the confidence to claim what is rightfully ours. We are our own biggest cheerleaders, and we can cheerfully pave the way for a future filled with triumph and fulfilment.

The trap lies in questioning your worthiness when good things come your way, asking yourself, "Why me?" And when bad things occur, you find yourself stuck in the same mindset. This habit transforms positive moments into sources of self-doubt, hindering your growth and progress.

Remember, negativity attracts negativity.

A constant "Why me?" attitude will likely keep positive experiences at bay. Self-advocacy is not easy, but it is necessary. Everyone faces challenges, but those who feel deserving, who embrace positivity and self-belief, and who acknowledge their hard work tend to attract more good in their lives. They stand up for themselves, which is empowering.

Without actively promoting yourself, armed with hard facts and irrefutable evidence, you are less likely to get ahead. It is about moving from a negative, self-doubting mindset to a positive, self-assured one.

True worthiness or "deservingness" is grounded in facts and achievements, not just feelings. Base your self-worth on tangible successes rather than emotions.

The "Why me?" mindset is emotional; "Why not me?" is factual. Embracing this fact-based approach is key to stepping into your power and realizing your full potential.

Self-Preservation

Once you have started stepping into your power, you realize the need to protect yourself. Self-preservation is not just a survival instinct; it is your inner rudder in life's storms. It turns the unbearable into something you can weather, adapting your pace as needed.

Everyone's resilience has its own meter. My high tolerance for stress was forged early, shaped by academic and athletic challenges. My parents equipped my siblings and me with stress-busting tools like exercise and mindfulness, which are important in managing the pressures of life.

Self-preservation is not just a safety net. It is your lifeline. Lose it, and recovery will be a steep climb. This instinct rebalances your life, helping you recalibrate what truly matters: your core values and your sources of joy.

Life has taught me the invaluable lesson of patience, a skill that I consider to be indispensable. Throughout my personal journey, I have realized that great achievements are not rushed. As they say, "Rome was not built in a day." Pursuing excellence requires a steadfast and patient demeanor, serving as the cornerstone of lasting success.

Preserve yourself. This is a fight-or-flight situation.

Tolerance Levels

This is a good moment to consider your tolerance levels.

Reflect on your emotional capacity to manage feelings, memories, and physical sensations tied to specific issues and situations. Each of us has a tolerance threshold. Within this threshold, we can remain open and receptive; however, once we step beyond it, we become reactive.

Throughout each day, we navigate within our tolerance threshold based on our activities and emotions. Our responses are influenced by our mental and physical well-being, as well as our emotional state—whether we are content, hungry, fatigued, or irritable. These factors collectively shape our ability to handle unforeseen circumstances, adapt to change, or cope with disappointment while maintaining our functionality.

Reflecting on this will enhance your self-awareness of your

tolerance levels, enabling you to make adjustments when you exceed your comfort zone.

Ideally, we should aim to live within our tolerance levels, remaining composed amid pressure and stress. When our tolerance is tested, we may feel overwhelmed, triggering our nervous systems into fight-or-flight mode. We might freeze, become emotionally and physically numb, or react negatively. Recognizing when we exceed our tolerance boundaries is crucial.

Tolerance levels vary among individuals and evolve with time and life experiences. For example, a woman going through menopause may experience lower levels of tolerance than women who are not.

Let's take a look at how positive and negative memories play into our tolerance levels.

Recall a time when you maintained composure amid stress. Detail the scenario: What triggered it? What thoughts ran through your mind at that instant, and how did you manage to stay composed under pressure? Did your reaction lead to a positive or negative outcome? Upon contemplation, was the incident significant in the grand scheme of things?

Now recall a moment when you surpassed your usual tolerance limits. What signs indicated you ventured beyond your comfort zone? Did you feel disconnected from the people around you? Were you emotionally distant? How did your body respond, and how did you react? What were the consequences of your actions? Capture your insights.

By identifying the catalysts of our unease, we empower ourselves to promptly realign within our threshold.

Everyone needs a way forward, a way to survive when you find yourself in a place beyond what you can tolerate. I recommend this: Trust your body and intuition to signal when things become overwhelming. Pause, count to ten if possible, take a deep breath, and collect yourself before responding. If needed, step away. If a response is necessary, stay calm and address the situation rationally.

Integrate moments of mindfulness into your daily routine to enhance mental resilience, as life will always present challenges.

No Quick Fixes

Some of us have a fighting spirit, while others may struggle and crumble under pressure. Understanding your own disposition is vital. Regardless, the ultimate goal is to reclaim control of your life and rise above the challenges.

Not everyone possesses inherent strength, but if you have even a trace of it, that is what you must harness to pause, reflect, recharge, and propel yourself forward.

Rebuilding yourself is not a quick fix. It involves extinguishing the fires, dusting off the ashes, and recognizing there is something solid to work with. It is a journey toward reclaiming control of your life.

Getting to this point often means actively listening to what others are saying and seeing your situation for what it is. There will come a time when you cannot ignore the issues anymore. You have to change, or you will end up burnt to a crisp.

Sometimes, people need to hit rock bottom, burn right down, and then rise again, stronger than before, like a phoenix rising from the ashes. The real fighters are those who, despite looking burnt out on the outside, still scrape off the burnt bits to find who they are underneath.

They see their pain, know they deserve better, and do not just aim to survive. They want to thrive. This means embracing self-care and making changes that are really about looking after themselves. It is all up to you. You have a choice.

But if you ignore what you are feeling, you are setting yourself up for a fall.

When burnout looms, your only choice might be to surrender and seek help. But with self-awareness, you can avoid that brink. Be mindful of your internal alarms, remain vigilant, and don't allow the world's chaos to drown out your inner compass. This force isn't just about holding on; it's about changing the game. It serves as both your lifeline and catalyst for transformation.

Neglect it, and you'll become crisp beyond redemption.

Recognize the early signs, nurture self-awareness, and commit to a path that leads to balance and fulfilment. That is the game plan.

Personal Stress-Awareness Exercise

Stress is something we all face, but it touches each of us in unique ways. To tackle stress effectively, it's crucial to recognize how it manifests in our lives. Start by asking yourself: How do I behave under stress? What does stress mean to me? What do I look like when I'm stressed out? Scan the QR code in Figure 4.2 to learn more about stress awareness.

Identify your stress signals. Pay attention to your physical, emotional, and behavioral responses to stress. Common signs include physical tension, reacting strongly in tough situations, feeling overwhelmed or incapable, troubles with sleep, or

Figure 4.2. How to recognize stress and how it affects you

overindulging. By identifying your personal stress signals, you'll become more attuned to when it's time to set boundaries and take care of yourself!

Identify your stress triggers. Once you've pinpointed your personal stress signals, it's time to uncover your stress triggers. These can range from financial worries to an overload of responsibilities, whether at work or home, or even the end of a relationship or an illness. By understanding what sets off your stress, you can proactively prepare for these situations and set boundaries in advance to keep overwhelm at bay.

Craft a self-care plan. After you've identified your stress signs and triggers, crafting a self-care plan becomes essential. Think of activities like exercising, meditating, spending time in nature, ensuring you get enough sleep, or diving into deep breathing exercises. By weaving self-care into your daily life, you'll be better prepared to tackle tough moments and set boundaries whenever necessary. Embrace these practices and watch as you navigate challenges with newfound resilience.

PART TWO

Looking Out for Number One

CHAPTER 5

Self-Care

Too often, we disregard our own survival instincts, entangling ourselves in the intricate web of life's external pressures. We deceive ourselves with the notion of, "I've got this," yet the truth is, we frequently find ourselves out of our depth. This self-deception leads us to do something dangerous: neglect our self-care. Believing that we can dismiss the inward and outward signs of burnout is a catastrophic miscalculation.

Many of us find ourselves caught in a vicious cycle of disregarding signs of burnout, enduring absurdities, stretching ourselves thin, and acquiescing even when we yearn to decline.

Without exceptional leadership, identifying burnout becomes a blind spot, and we deceive ourselves into believing that we can persevere.

We find ourselves amid a profound shift in leadership, diversity, and societal norms. If you're passively observing this, you become part of the scenery. To navigate this whirlwind, you must remain sharp, or you risk being sidelined and burned out. While these changes may seem overwhelming, they demand our attention. The transformation is unstoppable. Our very existence must be reevaluated to thrive in this period of upheaval.

We are gearing up for battle. So suit up, ladies.

Put on Your Armor

Prioritize yourself. You need to be in top form to leverage the changes in your favor and combat the ones resisting equity and social progress. If we do not look after ourselves, it will all crumble.

Self-care is our armor in the battle of life, a vital defense against its relentless grind. It involves actively nurturing our mental, physical, and emotional well-being, and recognizing its nonnegotiable importance.

We must be mindful of its daily impact on our lives, as neglecting it can result in a gradual decline in our efficiency, health, and overall quality of life. Prioritize self-care and reap the benefits it brings.

This might seem like a small thing, but scheduling regular breaks, not just when you are at your limit, is the key to avoiding total burnout. It is about catching those moments of mental, physical, or emotional strain early.

An Australian study in 2021 looked into just this issue, and found that there are indeed "restorative benefits of short breaks and vacations."[19]

If you are imagining smoke and fire, as we discussed in the previous chapters, this would be about small fires. Address them immediately, and they won't lead to a loss of control.

You need to notice immediately when you feel uncomfortable about something. Do not simply shrug it off as "part of the job." (If the #MeToo movement taught us anything, it definitely taught us that!)

Many times, we accept various discomforts simply because we believe it's just the way things are. However, this mindset can be deceptive. It begins with a small hint of pain that we must acknowledge promptly. Ignoring such signals never leads to positive outcomes. In fact, it fosters within us a tolerance for mistreatment.

You might even start thinking that being overworked and underpaid is just part of life. But that's nonsense. We must challenge and reject the toxic belief that the mistreatment of

---

[19] Jan Packer, "Taking a Break: Exploring the Restorative Benefits of Short Breaks and Vacations," *Annals of Tourism Research Empirical Insights* 2, no. 1 (2021), https://doi.org/10.1016/j.annale.2020.100006.

women in the workplace is simply an accepted reality. Let us rise above this mindset and work toward a more equitable and inclusive environment.

Authentic self-care goes beyond simply engaging in leisurely activities. It entails immersing yourself in endeavors that bring you joy with minimal effort. Cultivating meaningful relationships with loved ones, family, and friends is not only therapeutic but also crucial. Nurturing these connections fosters unwavering support and emotional well-being.

There are many ways to manage stress. Physical activity is a vital one—regular exercise. But you also need to maintain a healthy diet and prioritize adequate sleep. Practicing self-care also involves setting boundaries and learning to say no. It means resisting the urge to conform to external pressures.

Here's an example from my own life. During the lockdown, my business thrived, requiring increased dedication and effort. I found myself constantly connected to clients worldwide, spending countless hours in front of my screen. Unbeknownst to me, this took a toll on my well-being. Not only was I supporting clients through their pandemic-related stress and anxiety, but I was also juggling my own family dynamics.

Also, my husband did not cope well with the lockdown. Being a workaholic in the film industry, he was accustomed to staying incredibly busy and being constantly engaged in his work.

Self-Care

I bore the weight of his frustration, doing my best to shield our daughter from its impact. I absorbed all the stress while managing the daily household routines, including cooking and sharing the cleaning. Thankfully, my daughter was older, sparing me the additional responsibility of homeschooling.

Navigating life with a husband slipping into a dark place during the pandemic, all while managing my clients' concerns, proved to be an arduous task. I believed I possessed unwavering resilience, yet I underestimated the profound impact it would have on my mental and emotional well-being. Though I managed to incorporate some physical exercise into my routine, I remained oblivious to the detrimental effects of the mounting stress and anxiety on my psyche.

After the pandemic, my workload skyrocketed, and I found myself swamped with even more tasks. I love my work, and the rapid growth of my business was exhilarating. In fact, I always warn my clients about growing too fast! Yet there I was, caught in the same whirlwind.

By mid-November 2021, fatigue engulfed me. My vitality was drained, and interacting with clients became an ordeal. I came to the realization that I had taken on more than I could handle. The truth dawned on me: I had stretched myself too thin, and navigating through to Christmas would require immense effort.

I managed to push through, but as soon as my final client left, I collapsed. I found myself confined to bed, battling a serious illness, and feeling completely depleted. Overwhelmed by anxiety and the weight of others' stress, I was left utterly drained. I thought, "This is it. I'm teetering on the edge of burnout."

That is when the idea for this book hit me.

That moment served as a profound wake-up call, revealing the stealthy and pervasive nature of burnout. Despite recognizing the warning signs and feeling the strain, I stubbornly convinced myself that I could manage. I continued to run my own business, donning the cape of Superwoman.

I guess I had to learn the hard way. Luckily, it happened during a downtime when most people were off work. I was in desperate need of a genuine break, a break that would truly rejuvenate me. So I pushed my January commitments to February, carving out a six-week break for myself.

It boils down to this: If you are not looking out for yourself, who will? You are all you've got. You have to be your own pillar of strength and kindness. A support system is great, but in the end, it is all on you.

Self-care, coming from genuinely loving yourself and respecting your boundaries, is what fuels you and will make you happy. If you want to give your best, nourish yourself first.

A Self-Care Check-In

Caring for yourself is equally important as caring for others. By showing self-compassion, kindness, and care, you reflect the respect you have for yourself and establish standards for how others should treat you. Self-care isn't just a concept but should be an integral part of your daily life. It can manifest in various ways, whether through a relaxing spa day, self-indulgence, or quality time spent with cherished friends. Instead of solely focusing on meeting others' expectations, prioritize your own needs.

According to the International Self-Care Foundation, there are seven pillars of self-care. These seven pillars collaborate harmoniously to form a comprehensive framework. They encompass these seven domains of well-being: mental, emotional, physical, environmental, spiritual, recreational, and social.[20]

Let's assess your current self-care routines and discover ways to enhance them. How well do you prioritize caring for yourself? Consider the following questions to see how you stack up.

How are you caring for your mental health?

- Practicing mindfulness
- Journaling

---

20 International Self-Care Foundation, "Empowering Holistic Well-Being," accessed October 25, 2024, https://isfglobal.org/about-isf/.

- Engaging in talk therapy
- Taking tech breaks
- Learning something new

What are you doing to support your emotional health?

- Dumping your energy drainers
- Pausing for reflection
- Asking for help when needed
- Limiting negative self-talk
- Setting boundaries

How are you treating your body?

- Eating regular, nourishing meals
- Exercising regularly
- Getting enough sleep
- Drinking plenty of water

Are you nourishing your soul (spirituality)?

- Practicing gratitude
- Listening to music
- Reading
- Volunteering
- Meditating

Are you making time for fun (recreation)?

- Going on adventures
- Partaking in a hobby
- Chilling out
- Learning a new language
- Traveling

Are you engaging socially?

- Going out for dinner/drinks with friends
- Staying in touch with family
- Participating in group activities
- Making a contribution to a board or community venture

These holistic approaches all contribute to your self-care. If you can check off a couple of ideas in seven pillars, you're on track. If not, it's time to step up and put in the effort to elevate your self-care routine.

Putting Out the Fire

As we delve into the realms of self-awareness and burnout, we are confronted with an unmistakable scent of smoke. This scent serves as a metaphor for the initial signs of personal and professional overwhelm.

It all starts with a lingering question: "Am I the only one feeling this way?" The answer to this question becomes your cue. When you catch that first whiff of trouble, swift action is crucial. These early signs, much like a simmering flame, have the potential to rapidly escalate into a raging blaze of stress.

Waking up with a sense of dread, staying in the office long past dinnertime, feeling too exhausted to prepare a meal, or experiencing sudden spikes of anxiety—each of these are not mere routine hiccups; rather, they are vivid red flags demanding your attention.

The initial spark is often the result of multiple factors that gradually intensify into a burn. It could be the consequence of saying yes when you should have said no, or the feeling of being undervalued and overlooked in your professional life.

It is the insidious nature of these small, accumulating incidents that erode your well-being over time. You may not react immediately, but eventually, you come to the realization that something has gone awry.

Rejection and failure are part of life. When you experience them, each setback should be a learning experience and sharpen your awareness.

Be in the moment and feel it. If something is off, change it.

Self-Care

The Power of Sharing Stories

At the Pipeline in London, where the focus is on supporting ambitious women, my good friend and colleague, Karen Mackley, and I often host three-day learning and development summits for leaders from both the public and the private sectors. It is during these events that we see a common challenge among them—imposter syndrome. These remarkable women, burdened with overwhelming responsibilities, often find themselves overlooked for well-deserved promotions. However, it is through the power of coming together that they realize they are not alone in their struggles.

Opening up and realizing "it's not just me" is a powerful start. It shatters the illusion of isolation. Often, we blame ourselves, thinking we are the issue. But the truth is, it is a shared struggle.

Speaking out and sharing your story is more than a catharsis. It is an invitation for others to rally with you. We need this unity, especially as women. As I always say, collective strength is our ally. So talk it out and build a support network. By sharing and listening, you gain perspective.

You will find your story echoed in the stories of others. This awareness that you are part of a larger narrative dispels loneliness. It is imperative to understand that you are not in this alone.

Breaking free from isolation begins to ease the burden. It is a step toward extinguishing those initial sparks before they are a full-blown crisis.

Daily Recovery

Rather than waiting for a crisis to create a major intervention, small, ongoing actions can keep you balanced.

Recent research suggests that several short breaks throughout the year are more beneficial than a single, long vacation. It is about regular decompression instead of waiting for a holiday to unwind from accumulated stress.

We often find ourselves in a pre-vacation frenzy, racing to finish the tasks with the promise of relaxation on the horizon. But why not adopt more frequent, shorter breaks to maintain headspace?

A stretched perspective from continuous stress and anxiety can be mitigated with brief, regular pauses. Perhaps opt for a week off annually, in addition to taking several extended weekends. Of course, make sure you truly disconnect.

Incorporate mindful moments into your daily routine. Even two minutes dedicated to a simple breathing exercise, like the 4-6-4 pattern, can significantly reduce stress.

Recognize when anxiety or impatience mounts and allow

yourself a pause. Count to ten, breathe deeply, and think before reacting.

Think about recovering daily. This is also about starting your day right, whether it is with a nourishing breakfast or a routine that revitalizes you. It is these small, daily actions that keep us functioning optimally.

For those who procrastinate or thrive under pressure, daily self-care might not come naturally. But it is crucial. The aim is not just to survive until the last minute, but to manage stress gradually and consistently. Ask for help when you need it! It is not a weakness. It is smart self-management.

Also, consider the role of technology. Putting down your phone and stepping away from social media can be incredibly freeing. Social media often pushes us into unhealthy comparisons and sets unrealistic expectations, adding unnecessary stress.

Be realistic about your daily goals and limits. True self-awareness comes from regularly tuning out the noise and tuning in to moments of stillness and reflection.

Take a Moment Out

Here's a wonderful way to carve out a moment of self-care. Craft a personal mantra that bolsters a positive outlook. This mantra can guide you in being a kinder companion to yourself, nurturing empathy and compassion for both yourself and others. Concentrate on empathy, gentleness, inner resilience, and maintain a deliberate personal focus.

By setting a positive intention, like striving to be a force for good, we infuse our lives with energy and purpose. Repeating your mantra can soothe your mind and strengthen your beliefs. These positive feelings enhance your happiness, while moments of quiet nurture inner peace and security, alleviating loneliness and fear.

Mindful meditation takes practice. It's normal for your mind to wander; so don't dwell on self-criticism. When it does, just acknowledge it and return to your incantation.

Creating a Mantra Moment

Choose a comfortable sitting position that suits you best. Whether it's a chair or a cushion on the floor, go with what feels most comfortable. You can even lean back slightly as long as your spine, neck, and head are aligned in a straight line.

Centering attention on your breath is a straightforward practice. Simply notice the subtle sensations of air as it enters and exits your nostrils. If your mind wanders, gently redirect your focus back to the breath.

During meditation, aim to remain physically still. Also, focus on keeping your closed eyelids motionless. Pause to truly grasp the essence of each phrase. Feel free to repeat any that require clarity. Concentrate on your desires and aspirations, not just the outcomes.

As you conclude the exercise, consider silently repeating the following phrases in contemplative stillness:

> I am a force for good.
> I am a force for change.
> I am a force to be reckoned with.

This is my personal mantra. Repeating these words always makes me feel like a queen.

Connecting

In this era of digital overload, we have lost sight of the power of face-to-face interactions, the warmth of someone's presence, and the simple act of touching and being fully present with another person.

We have drifted from the core of genuine companionship, where sharing life's ups and downs face-to-face matters. Authentic conversations, where you genuinely engage and share with someone you care about, are the bedrock of deep relationships.

This kind of presence provides necessary comfort. It is a

lifeline, a crucial aspect of our well-being that includes self-care and mutual support.

As we increasingly mesh with technology, we blur the lines between reality and the digital facade. Sure, tech is groundbreaking, but it is also a massive distraction. There is more to life than scrolling, texting, or getting lost on LinkedIn, Instagram, Facebook, and TikTok. It is vital to disconnect from constant notifications and really connect with the world around us.

The power of human touch, like a twenty-second hug, is unmatched in its ability to reduce stress. It is a deep expression of our need for love, friendship, and comfort. Connection is a gift, both given and received, and it can transform your day.

Hug someone every day. It works both ways. We all need random acts of kindness.

Work It

We all know what is good for us, but there is often a gap between knowing and doing.

We are drawn to what is bad for us, like salty and sugary foods, despite health risks. And everything is okay in moderation, even your KFC fix. It's okay to indulge in guilty pleasures without forgetting that our body is our ultimate tool and our personal temple. But if you neglect your body, and your health inevitably crumbles, it will leave you unable to enjoy the activities and passions that bring joy and meaning to your life.

As a former elite athlete, I know the discipline exercise instills. This has served me well into my middle age. I'm thankful for my muscle memory every day!

But let's be real. High-intensity workouts at my age? No, thanks. Not happening.

So let's get practical. My routine now is to have twenty minutes of Pilates, weights or power plate, and walking. I do what my body allows me to do without hurting myself. This is my way of thanking my body and keeping it from breaking down. Sure, these activities won't stop arthritis, but I am healthy and still fitting into my twenty-year-old clothes. I'm certainly doing something right.

You have to love your vessel enough to care for it. Exercise does not have to be a high-impact ordeal. It is about mindfulness and loving yourself in those moments.

Change your perspective. Do not see it as a chore, but as a chance to be present and focused. Twenty minutes can leave you feeling rejuvenated.

I always feel better post-exercise. It is a recharge for endorphins, mental clarity, and staying in touch with myself. All of it is a defense against burnout.

So stay sharp. Understand what works for you and what doesn't. Focus on what nurtures you and dump the energy drainers.

Do not fear change. Sometimes, it is the very thing you need.

The Power of No

Have you ever caught yourself blurting out a yes when your gut screams no?

I've said this before, and I'll say it again and again. We need to think about the power of saying no. After impulsively uttering that yes, you question, "Why in the world did I agree to that?" It feels like a moment of madness.

Suddenly, you're grappling with unnecessary stress and anxiety, trying to fit in commitments that don't even excite you.

"No" is an immensely powerful and liberating word. Embrace it!

But it's not just about voicing it outwardly; it's also an internal battle. Embracing your inner "no" is about establishing healthy boundaries. When faced with an uncertain request, take a pause. Reflect on it to gain a broader perspective before committing.

We often say yes out of fear—fear of appearing difficult, unhelpful, or disrupting the harmony. But it is essential to be

Self-Care

comfortable with not being universally liked if it means staying true to ourselves.

If you genuinely don't want to do something, confidently say no without hesitation. Do not allow your inner voice to hinder you.

It's perfectly all right to take some time to do nothing. Embracing guilt-free relaxation is just as essential as completing any task.

Allow yourself those moments of peace without self-reproach. "No" is about drawing lines and asserting your worth. "No" is more than a word. It is a shield against burnout. It's a declaration of self-care.

In a world that demands your "yes," let "no" be your powerful ally. Scan the QR code in Figure 5.1 for tips on how to get better at saying no.

Embrace the practice of self-care as a powerful expression of self-love and respect. Stand up against unfair treatment,

Figure 5.1. How to say no

seek assistance when needed, and remember that resilience has limits. Ignoring your own needs will only lead to burnout.

By prioritizing self-care, you demonstrate your confidence and commitment to your well-being in the long run. It is an investment in yourself, sending a clear message to others that you are self-aware, attuned to your needs, and unafraid to put yourself first.

Remember, placing yourself at the top of your to-do list is not selfish, but rather a necessary act of self-care that enables you to show up as your best self.

CHAPTER 6

Self-Criticism

It is disheartening to witness highly accomplished women undervalue their success by attributing it to luck or timing, rather than acknowledging their own determination and talent. As I have previously discussed in this book, this ingrained sense of not deserving success, prevalent in our society, traps us in a cycle of self-doubt and questioning whether we are worthy of our achievements.

There have been numerous instances where I have felt like an outsider, especially as the only Black woman in predominantly White spaces. However, the feeling of being undeserving is distinct.

During my upbringing, my parents ensured I saw people like myself represented in various contexts. As a result, despite feeling out of place at times, I never questioned my right to be there. My parents instilled in me the belief that I deserved every opportunity just as much as anyone else, especially those in privileged positions.

This upbringing ensured that my mindset was not wondering, "Why me?" but confidently asserting, "Why not me?," as noted previously.

I am blessed to have a family that has made me feel loved and worthy. This affirmation has wielded a profound influence over my life, serving as a driving force for my aspirations and achievements.

Early on, I noticed many women lacked the self-worth I was raised with. My friends, even those who seemed to have everything, battled insecurities and questioned their privileges, unlike their male counterparts, who rarely did.

As I entered university, I noticed a growing divide. I encountered a wealthy girl at Dartmouth, my alma mater, who was cloaked in luxury, from limos to lynx coats. However, beneath her extravagant facade lay deep insecurities, not genuine self-assurance. Gradually, it became evident that her privilege served as a shield, protecting her from the realities of life.

Fulfilling Our Potential

Let's take a closer look at life in the 2020s, where we continue to grapple with issues such as unequal pay, underrepresentation

Self-Criticism

of women in CEO positions, and limited female political leadership. It is disheartening that the United States has yet to see a female president, and the UK's count of only two female prime ministers, including the controversial case of Liz Truss, leaves much to be desired. This reality undermines our confidence and faith in what is truly achievable.

Certainly, I have experienced my fair share of ups and downs, but unlike many women, my moments of uncertainty have not stemmed from profound doubt, but rather from circumstance. My primary focus remains on fulfilling my potential.

During my time in the television industry, I earned the nickname "Diva Blades" because of my insistence on excellence and attention to detail. However, it is important to clarify that I have never exhibited diva-like behavior. For me, it's all about cultivating an atmosphere of respect and professionalism in the workplace. That does not exclude creating an atmosphere of happiness, openness, and collective drive for the greater good of everyone involved.

I do my job well because I'm driven and passionate about people, and it aligns with my purpose, helping others and myself fulfill our potential. It is not about ego, but about giving what I have to give when needed.

Self-doubt sows the seed of fear, rendering us paralyzed by the anxiety of not measuring up. It confines us to a prison of negative thinking, stifling our capacity to seize opportunities and confront challenges. It is not solely the fear of failure, but also the dread of how failure affects us emotionally.

Shifting from "I can't" to "I can," or from "Why me?" to "Why not me?" is surprisingly straightforward. It involves reshaping those repetitive negative thoughts that hold us back.

When women doubt themselves, the world misses out on correcting injustice and inequality and challenging the status quo. Women possess unique strengths such as emotional intelligence, relationship building, and empathy, all of which are essential in today's world.

By marginalizing ourselves and denying our place at the forefront of change, we are inevitably heading toward disaster. It's time to fully embrace our capabilities and contributions to shaping a better future.

Women must stand together and uplift underrepresented groups. The true strength lies within our collective efforts.

Practicing the Practical

There are many ways to combat damaging self-criticism. One of my favorites is to document your strengths.

Self-Criticism

Five Signature Strengths Exercise

Take fifteen minutes to discover your five signature strengths. We all possess them, yet rarely take the time to acknowledge their presence.

Jot down those five remarkable abilities that define you, supported by concrete examples. For future global leaders, below are some competencies that are considered crucial. Choose your top five strengths from the list below. Don't worry if you can't come up with five; three strengths would be solid for a middle manager, while five would be expected from an established leader.

Emotional intelligence

Communication

Courageous

Collaborative

Appreciating diversity

Thinking globally

Resilience

Flexibility

Strategic thinking

Vision

Change management

Integrity

Empowering others

Innovative

Avoid generic statements like, "I'm a great communicator," or "I'm an excellent organizer." Instead, provide specific instances that exemplify your strengths. These examples are undeniable evidence of your superpowers, preventing you from downplaying your accomplishments.

In our fast-paced and stressful world, we often forget to take a moment to acknowledge our own accomplishments. When you find yourself overwhelmed, frustrated, and doubting your impact, pause and reflect on what you have achieved. Open your notebook and witness your capabilities in black-and-white. This will fuel your fire. And, that's why it's crucial to document your successes.

Positive Reinforcement Exercise

I work with many successful women who struggle with self-criticism and repetitive negative thinking. To help them overcome these patterns, I provide them with a simple exercise to reprogram their mindset.

To begin, start by maintaining a three-day diary in which you document each occurrence of negative thoughts and their corresponding triggers. It is crucial to comprehend these triggers, as they play a pivotal role in reversing such detrimental thought patterns. These negative thoughts might have their roots in childhood experiences, deeply ingrained negative beliefs, or personal setbacks. Regardless of their origin, identifying these triggers is imperative to addressing and reshaping the negative thinking process.

By bringing awareness to these patterns and understanding their origins, we can work toward replacing them with more positive and empowering thoughts.

Transform your virtues into visual reminders by placing uplifting statements on Post-it notes in locations you frequent daily: your night table, bathroom mirror, laptop, and refrigerator door, to name a few. Commit to this practice for a month and witness the transformative power of positive reinforcement on your mindset. Over time, repeating affirming thoughts will gradually replace the negative ones, bringing about a profound shift in your perspective.

Nourishment

Caring for your mind, body, and soul is vital to your personal perspective. The concept of self-care encompasses our actions to sustain ourselves during challenging times and uplift our spirits.

It's important to see self-care as nourishment, not only through the food we eat but also through the music we listen to, the books we read, the art and scenery we appreciate, and the meaningful conversations we engage in. Engaging in these activities nurtures our senses and keeps us grounded in the grand scheme of things. They allow us to escape the cycle of overthinking and self-analysis, preventing exhaustion and burnout while promoting overall well-being.

For me, cooking is the ultimate source of stimulation and stress relief. After a tiring day at work, the mere act of chopping ingredients helps me release tension, redirecting that energy into creating something delicious. It's a form of nourishment that transcends mere sustenance, nurturing not only my body but also my soul.

Consider trying some of the following.

- Recall a conversation or interaction that profoundly enriched your soul. What was the subject of discussion? Who were you engaged with? It could have been an engaging dialogue with close friends or colleagues, exploring a topic of immense significance to all of you. Perhaps it left you feeling serene, enlightened, or invigorated.

- Next, reflect on a conversation or interaction that left you feeling depleted. Perhaps you experienced a sense of being diminished during that encounter.

You can apply this exercise to different facets of your life. Think about the music you listen to, the books and articles you read, what you choose to focus on (including your appearance and physical health), and of course, your dietary choices. By being mindful of these decisions, you can enrich your overall experience and well-being.

Ways to Nourish and Unwind

Nourishing my mind and creative spirit is as crucial as dealing with clients' problems. As an executive coach, I am constantly absorbing others' issues, so finding a release is essential, and this is why I avoid long phone conversations.

To find solace, I retreat to the countryside for a peaceful walk, immersing myself in the serenity and allure of nature. Additionally, I indulge in the guilty pleasure of binge-watching shows like "Love Is Blind" or "Married at First Sight: Australia." Don't judge me; I'm not the only one! These social phenomena offer a much-needed mental respite, allowing me to unwind without any cognitive effort, simply drifting away.

I derive nourishment from anything that ignites creativity, be it exceptional music or captivating art. These experiences enrich my soul, broaden my perspectives, and foster an appreciation for diversity.

Nourishment extends beyond food and encompasses physical activities and self-care. Engaging in exercise and treating yourself to a relaxing spa day can provide a much-needed rejuvenation. Home massages, chakra alignments, and reflexology treatments offer a unique recalibration of energy that daily routines can't replicate. Embracing these revitalizing practices is a wonderful way to prioritize your well-being.

The nourishment for the soul lies in giving back, which can take various forms, such as charity work, serving on boards, volunteering, or simple acts of kindness. Personally, I am involved with two amazing organizations: New Curators, which aims to diversify the art world by showcasing underrepresented talent, and Creative Access, which strives to promote diversity in the world of media. Engaging with these young, ambitious individuals from diverse backgrounds brings me immense joy. Giving back this way brings me unparalleled fulfilment.

Even a simple, friendly exchange on the street can nourish you. Time and again, this basic act will show the power of kindness.

In today's harsh world, choosing to be genuinely nice (not a doormat, but a decent human being) will truly differentiate you.

The bottom line? Change your mindset. Make sure to prioritize things properly, set boundaries, and uplift yourself. This is the key to nurturing self-esteem and empowerment, instead of succumbing to self-criticism. You've got this!

Self-Criticism

Talk to Someone

Sharing our problems can be challenging, as we often worry about burdening others. However, consider how frequently you've been a listening ear for those around you. It's all about the reciprocity of positive energy and good karma payback.

You can overcome feelings of unworthiness by connecting with someone you deeply trust, someone who recognizes your abilities and truly understands your value. Receiving positive affirmation from a friend or family member who genuinely appreciates your worth is the first step toward conquering these emotions.

Having a confidant offers a sense of safety and a reassuring safety net. They are the ones who will remind you of your worth.

Nevertheless, it is crucial to exercise caution, as certain individuals may take advantage of this bond and exhibit selfish tendencies.

Don't let negativity from others consume you or drain your energy. Remember the wise words of Mary J. Blige: "No more drama."

Avoid getting entangled in needless drama. When you genuinely need support, turn to someone you trust and have a close bond with. If that's not available, remember that professionals like therapists and counselors are there to listen, ready to offer their expertise. Alternatively, a physical outlet like a punching bag can work wonders!

For women, carrying burdens has become almost second nature. Regardless of our achievements, we bear the weight of daily life, often without receiving the recognition we deserve.

That's our role: to carry the burden, to shoulder the lion's share of everyday responsibilities without reaping all the rewards. We are the ones who put in the hard work, who take care of household chores, and who step up as breadwinners.

We are expected to handle it all, while sometimes finding it bewildering that some men struggle with basic everyday household tasks.

However, it is unrealistic to assume that we can bear the weight of all these responsibilities without any outlet. Suppressing problems inevitably leads to disastrous explosions. Try to regularly release these pent-up emotions and prevent them from building up. Instead, address issues in manageable portions.

Talking it out is more than just unloading. It is a chance to pause, reflect, and gain clarity. It is an essential respite in the chaos of daily life.

Avoid Energy Vampires

To rid yourself of negative energy, start by removing any "energy vampires" from your life. These individuals deplete your strength, sow self-doubt by making you question your judgment, and divert your focus from personal growth. These people manipulate or feed off those willing to lend an ear and offer support. It's no surprise that they often target those who are sensitive and compassionate and see the good in others more than in themselves.

The detrimental effects of energy vampires arise from their capacity to perpetuate chronic stress. This is especially noticeable when the energy vampire happens to be someone you can't easily distance yourself from, such as a spouse, parent, or boss. Consistently having your energy drained by these individuals becomes a significant source of stress.

When it comes to safeguarding your own energy and well-being from energy vampires, remember, it's not selfishness; it's practicing excellent self-care.

Here are a few ways to get rid of your bloodsuckers:

- *Cut them out of your life.* If they're not someone you can't avoid (such as a boss or a family member), limit contact with the person. Communicate as little as possible and use technology to your advantage by texting instead of picking up a phone call.
- *If you must communicate, establish clear boundaries.* Understand which activities are effective and which ones are not, and plan accordingly.

- *Find excuses not to engage.* Tell your energy vampire you're sick or tired. They will quickly find someone else to indulge them.

- *Don't lose the plot.* This will frequently trigger your energy vampire to respond in kind, resulting in feelings of self-doubt and negativity.

- *Just say no.* Declining with a simple no is a statement of great power. It is possible to convey this response kindly and respectfully, without being impolite. Everyone has the ability to exemplify empathy and compassion while asserting themselves. Remember, when you remove toxic individuals from your life, you will experience a surge of positivity and renewed energy.

Now that you've removed the negativity, you have room for more positivity. It's time to take stock.

I firmly believe in the immense power of manifestation. However, it requires creating space, embracing light, cultivating energy, and fostering openness for it to manifest in your life.

One way to do this is to get moving. Even if it is only a simple walk or an hour-long gym session, find what releases your stress.

My mama sent me a "Dammit Doll," a little (ungendered) rag doll for those frustrating moments when I just want to slap someone. Slamming it against anything is quite surprisingly cathartic, and no one gets hurt. Whatever works for you!

Channel Your Inner "Sasha Fierce"

Releasing negative energy can have a profound impact on your life, not only making you feel lighter but also fundamentally transforming how you process thoughts. Creating mental space for positivity enables you to recognize that things may not be as bleak as they seem and that you possess untapped strength and capability beyond what you give yourself credit for.

By shedding negativity, you create space in your mind to reconstruct your thought patterns. This transformation allows for greater clarity, enabling you to cultivate positive thinking and embrace a more empowered mindset.

Engaging in this process is like tapping into your inner "Sasha Fierce," a powerful alter ego Beyoncé uses to overcome her stage fright. This entails making a conscious choice to connect with the aspect of yourself that radiates positivity and resilience, rather than surrendering to self-doubt and negativity. If Beyoncé needs an alter ego, you might too. I have a power angel I channel whenever I'm giving a speech in front of a large audience or when I need to compel people into action. She's my courage counselor!

THE QUIET BURN

Within each of us resides an innate strength, a resounding voice that compels us to seize life's abundant opportunities, recognize our self-worth, and appreciate the distinct abilities and talents we possess. Whether it's our exceptional organizational skills, our indomitable spirit of motivation, or any other unique aptitude, we are empowered to embrace our fullest potential.

This shift in mindset is not merely a small adjustment in thinking; it is a powerful transformation that involves quieting the internal voice of doubt and amplifying the voices that recognize your true strength. It serves to fortify your belief in your capabilities and the distinctive contributions you are capable of making.

Here's an exercise to assess your own confidence.

- Take ten minutes to think about two or three people who you think exude confidence. What do you see? Notice their body language. How do they use their voice? Do you feel their presence?
- Do you have any of the same qualities? How can you use them better in the room?
- Describe in detail your own Sasha Fierce. Write it down for reference.
- Now think of something you want to say that you're afraid to say out loud. Bring your Sasha Fierce to life by

Self-Criticism

turning your inner ego out. With a partner or even in the mirror, practice fearlessly saying exactly what you want. Let her roar the first chance you get.

By embracing your inner Sasha Fierce, you not only enhance your self-confidence but also position yourself to make remarkable progress in all aspects of your life. It's about unlocking and embracing the guidance of your most empowered self, paving the way for personal growth and fulfilment.

Keep Your Perspective

Step away from your devices regularly. Social media is a minefield of negative messages, making you feel inadequate. From idealized images implying you need a makeover, to ads insinuating you are not good enough, these pervasive messages affect your self-perception.

When you look after yourself, when you buy into self-respect instead of just self-criticism, it will build a wholeness within you. It fills that space that was once negative with positivity. It builds your resistance and determination to be treated right by others, ensuring that your sacrifices are worthwhile and rooted in self-preservation. It will reorient your mind, body, and soul.

You have the choice. Embrace the good that you deserve, or

remain stuck in the same old negative loop, trapped in outdated mindsets about your worth.

It's time to rewrite your narrative. Discard the old, limiting beliefs. Set them on fire before they use you as kindling.

Life is too short to live any less than 100 percent. If you want a seat at the top table, to savor life rather than be consumed by it, invest in yourself. If not, you are just fuel for the fire.

Smell the smoke? That's you on the grill. Time to wake up. You are being slowly cooked by complacency. Stop the self-criticism that is burning you.

Break free and be the change.

Exercise: Shattering the Cycle of Unhelpful Thoughts

Our thoughts, emotions, and behaviors are like a dynamic trio, each constantly affecting the others. Sometimes, we fall into unhelpful thought patterns or habits that upset this balance. These can sway our feelings and, in turn, shape how we think and act, creating a tricky cycle. But here's the exciting part: We have the power to break this cycle and boost our mental health along the way! By taking charge of our thoughts and actions, we can transform our mental well-being.

Self-Criticism

Figure 6.1. How to recognize and deal with unhelpful thoughts

Swapping out negative thoughts for positive ones is a powerful way to tackle stress and anxiety, boost your sleep, and lift your spirits. As you make this a habit, you'll notice a remarkable improvement in your mental health and overall well-being. Scan the QR code in Figure 6.1 for more information on processing unhelpful thoughts.

Discovery. We often don't realize how our own unhelpful thoughts sneak into our minds, making them hard to catch. But once we learn to recognize these patterns, they become easier to spot. Here are some common culprits:

- Are you only seeing the negatives and ignoring the positives?
- Do you blame yourself entirely when things go wrong?
- Is your thinking black-and-white, seeing things as either perfect or disastrous?
- Do you always expect the worst in every situation?

By spotting these thought patterns, we can start turning the tide on them!

Compartmentalize negative thoughts. Catch those negative thoughts by keeping their categories in mind. Spot an unhelpful thought during your day? See if it fits into one of those categories. At first, tuning in to your thoughts may feel tricky, but simply being aware of the different types of negative thoughts will help you recognize when you're falling into them. As you keep reflecting and assessing, this process gets easier and can even become second nature over time.

Consider your viewpoint. Once you've spotted an unhelpful thought, assess it critically. Step back and look at the situation with fresh eyes. Instead of letting that thought drag you down, hit pause and give it a good evaluation. Ask yourself:

- How likely is that dreaded outcome, really?
- Do you have solid evidence backing it up?
- What other explanations or outcomes could there be?
- Could there be strong evidence for different perspectives on this situation?
- What advice would you offer a friend who was stuck in this thought loop?

Finally, take a moment to swap out that thought for one that's neutral or even positive. Reflect on the questions you

Self-Criticism

pondered while evaluating your thoughts and think about how you can reframe the situation. Imagine you're at work, and you could say: "I'm ready for this! I've poured in so much effort, and I'm going to give it my all," or "I've been rocking this role for a while now, nailing important tasks left and right, so there's no reason anyone would see me as anything but a success."

CHAPTER 7

Self-Compassion

You are not a machine. So don't treat yourself like one. You are not infallible. You are human, full of emotions and imperfections. And that is okay.

Self-compassion is the practice of treating yourself with kindness and understanding, instead of harsh self-criticism. It involves acknowledging your mistakes and failures with empathy, while still valuing and accepting yourself as a flawed but worthy individual.

I challenge you to honor your boundaries, cultivate a keen sense of self-awareness, and embrace the fact that you are a human being with limitations. As complex beings, we require moments of pause to fully immerse ourselves in the experience of life. Neglecting this necessity to embrace slowness deprives us of the pleasures that life has to offer.

Live in the moment, noticing and valuing each succeeding moment as it unfolds. This practice entails facing our emotions in the present moment, rather than postponing them with thoughts such as "I'll be fine once this is over" or "I'll prioritize my needs later." Without embracing this approach to self-compassion, we fail to grasp the essence of true happiness.

Failing to embrace our imperfections, vulnerabilities, and uniqueness leaves our existence empty. When we deny our humanity, we become mere automatons, devoid of the profound emotional spectrum that defines our human journey. Embracing our flaws and individuality is what truly enriches our lives.

Give yourself the grace to be flawed, to be real, and to be uniquely yourself.

If we can't allow ourselves to be human, be fallible, be vulnerable, and be different, then what is the point? You may as well be an Android bot.

Try replacing your constant self-critique (which we discuss in Chapter 6) with a simple yet powerful mantra: "I am enough."

Embracing this concept has the power to fundamentally transform your perspective. Genuine excellence cannot be attained without cultivating self-compassion.

Neglecting self-compassion, disregarding our emotional intelligence, or failing to comprehend our own emotions ultimately leaves us feeling empty. And what do we truly gain from this constant pressure we put on ourselves? Yes, we may achieve our goals, but often at the expense of our well-being, leaving us depleted and questioning the purpose of it all. As the late, great entertainer Peggy Lee poignantly asked, "Is that all there is?"

Dara's Story

I often think about my client Dara. Recently, Dara decided to step away from her role as senior vice president of marketing and communications at a world-renowned global giant, a position she found fulfilling and satisfying.

Previously, as VP of communications at another major media organization, Dara experienced severe burnout because of a toxic work environment combined with her unwavering commitment to excellence.

As an ethnic woman, she faced the harsh reality of racism and sexism daily. Although attempts were made to improve the company culture, entrenched and outdated systems made it challenging to bring about meaningful change. Despite receiving a promotion, Dara found herself expected to fulfill the responsibilities of two people, while also realizing that she was not receiving equal pay compared to her male counterparts. Overwhelmed and undervalued, she succumbed to the effects of both environmental and racial burnout.

THE QUIET BURN

At one point, Dara experienced a distressing incident in which her supervisor accused her of being passive-aggressive, leaving Dara feeling verbally attacked. The incident was traumatic. Subsequently, she reached out to HR to report the verbal attack and took time off from work to digest her experience. HR initiated a mediation process, during which the supervisor apologized. Consequently, her abuser was later fired.

Despite her exceptional capabilities, my client faced the challenges of micromanagement. She was unable to implement necessary staffing changes, all the while being expected to lead her team effectively. It soon became evident that Dara was set up for failure.

Being a marketing and communications leader, she was always on call, meeting deadlines and staying updated on breaking media events. Her exhaustion was tangible, and the relentless pressure exposed a profound sense of insecurity. Dara was working long hours, still completing the tasks at hand. She operated in a space where she was physically present but mentally absent. Dara functioned on autopilot, merely going through the motions because she felt she had to. The job and its financial rewards overshadowed her mental and physical well-being. Unwilling to feel defeated, she failed to recognize that she was her own worst enemy. And so Dara persisted within that hazy, smoke-filled space.

She recalled two challenging years of working sixty-hour weeks, always being available, and navigating the complex dynamics of workplace politics that come with being a Black woman in a predominantly White corporate setting. She pressed on, telling herself, "I can do this," but never pausing to ask, "Why?"

In retrospect, Dara wishes she had prioritized herself and advocated more fiercely on her own behalf. While she championed her team, she overlooked her own needs, becoming so worn down that she resigned herself to a toxic workplace culture, where chaos reigned and burnout prevailed. Sadly, her need to prove herself overshadowed her self-compassion.

In working with Dara, we focused on self-compassion and self-care. I encouraged her to let go of the need for constant perfection and to prioritize her well-being. We also worked on setting boundaries and effectively communicating her needs to higher management.

Nevertheless, it was only when she reached a breaking point that she realized something needed to change. Despite her self-awareness, she found herself teetering on the brink of an emotional collapse. This serves as a poignant reminder that burnout can catch anyone off guard, even those who are most in tune with themselves.

Your Manifesto

Caught in the relentless whirl of life, escaping from stress and chaos can be challenging. It can be tempting to keep pushing forward with blinders on, ignoring the warning signs. But when there is smoke, expect fire on its heels.

Let's be honest. Being talented and ambitious often leads to pushing oneself excessively. At times, the pressure can blur our boundaries, causing us to shoulder the burdens of others without asking ourselves, "Is this truly my responsibility?"

Taking a moment to reflect on why we instinctively assume these roles is critical. Embracing a healthy level of self-prioritization is not only important but essential. We must allow ourselves to be a bit selfish at times, as it directly affects our well-being. I propose not neglecting our duties, but rather prioritizing the creation of personal time that matches the energy we dedicate to others. Striking this equilibrium equals a life well lived.

Considering all of these aspects, it is important to recognize that self-compassion is synonymous with self-respect. By utilizing the self-care techniques discussed in Chapter 5, you can uplift yourself and cultivate a sense of profound self-esteem.

Self-Compassion

Self-care goes beyond mere routines; it entails taking responsibility for your well-being and engaging in activities that exemplify self-love and worthiness.

Engaging in self-care, be it through exercise, nourishing meals, or mindfulness practices, is a nurturing act of rebellion. It's a tangible expression of self-compassion that empowers you. In a world that constantly demands productivity, deliberately choosing activities that replenish your mind, body, and soul becomes a powerful form of personal resistance and self-validation.

I'm using personal manifesto language here because it's that important.

Rebel. Be radical. Resist. Then replenish.

So what's the point of this manifesto? Self-care should be woven into the fabric of our daily lives. If you don't look after yourself, who will?

At our core, we possess a profound understanding of ourselves. Our bodies, minds, and souls send signals when we push beyond our limits, yet regrettably, we often disregard these cues. Yet a key message that I hope resonated throughout the book is that neglecting self-care can have far-reaching consequences. When you prioritize others at the expense of yourself, it ultimately negatively affects both you and those around you.

Making your well-being a priority not only strengthens you

but also helps you find balance. It brings about a noticeable change in the way you carry yourself and radiates a sense of unwavering confidence.

Putting yourself first not only enhances your resilience but also has a profound impact on your interactions, fostering personal strength and social harmony. By nurturing yourself regularly, you undergo a transformative journey, moving through the world with reduced susceptibility to negativity and a determined sense of fortitude and resilience.

This requires self-devotion. It requires compassion. It requires sticking to your personal manifesto.

Rebel. Be radical. Resist. (Repeat.)

Stand Up for Yourself

If you don't stand up for yourself, people will take advantage of you. They'll think if you don't care, why should they? Not me. If someone is mistreating me, they're going to hear about it.

Here's an example of how I handle slow payers. Large corporations are frequently the culprits when it comes to delayed invoice payments. They often take up to ninety days to settle, resorting to tactics like requesting additional information or changes to invoice numbers. This behavior can be frustrating and time-consuming for suppliers—smaller entities like my coaching business.

Essentially, it's an admin nightmare. And that's the point: It's all part of the stalling technique.

I adopt a direct and straightforward approach. It is important to me, as a female business owner, that payments are made promptly in accordance with my invoice terms. The task of chasing invoices is both unpleasant and time-consuming, draining valuable energy. I always make my requests with courtesy, but let it be known that I am not hesitant to express myself directly.

Taking a firm stance is an integral aspect of self-compassion. It involves refusing to be burdened by the negligence of others. Late payments can be a source of inconvenience for both parties, and you have every right to assertively address the matter.

Big corporations especially should be expected to adhere to their financial obligations on time. There is no reason not to be unapologetic about saying, "Pay up."

Self-respect is about articulating your needs and standing up for yourself, holding your ground, and not giving in to a moment of hesitation to ask for what you rightfully deserve. You've earned it; you deserve it. End of story.

No doubt, prioritizing self-care is a crucial manifestation of self-compassion and savoring the rewards of your efforts—integral components of this practice. Unfortunately, women weigh themselves down with unwarranted guilt associated with these rewards.

It's time to liberate ourselves from this neglectful mindset and wholeheartedly embrace the significance of unapologetic self-care.

No Time for Guilt

Guilt can be a tremendous energy drain. Instead, firmly reject it with a resolute, "I don't have time for guilt." Grant yourself occasional luxuries, within your means, without any guilt.

Financial prudence is equally as important as relishing the rewards of your labor. Think of Ariana Grande's song "Seven Rings": "I see it, I like it, I want it, I got it."

Be it gourmet chocolates or gorgeous jewels, treat yourself according to your budget.

Many women frequently rely on others to pamper them, seeking external validation that goes against the very core of self-respect and self-empowerment. This dependence on external affirmation undermines the principle of self-compassion as a self-sufficient and fulfilling practice.

Claim what you deserve. As I always say, flip the script from "Why me?" to "Why not me?," and tell yourself, "I deserve this." These are absolutely necessary words for self-compassion.

"I deserve" is a declaration that opens the door to everything else. It instills a sense of adequacy, the root of self-compassion.

In those moments when you find yourself facing adversity alone, always remember: "God helps those who help themselves." This powerful reminder underscores the significance of being proactive in safeguarding your own well-being.

Your projection—how you present yourself to the outside world—shapes your reality. For example, a lack of self-compassion is evident in how you manage yourself. Perhaps you overcommit, work while unwell, or push yourself relentlessly without taking breaks. If this describes your behavior, don't expect compassion from others. The way you treat yourself teaches others how you want to be treated. This ultimately boils down to your own self-worth.

Many women begin their journey with confidence, but life's challenges can gradually erode that sense of self-worth. Reclaim that confidence by recognizing your inherent value, embracing your significance, and appreciating the profound impact you have through your mere presence.

Give Yourself What You Give Others

There is a fundamental balance between giving and receiving. Generosity is commendable, but it is equally important to allow yourself to be on the receiving end. Maintaining a healthy relationship requires a balanced exchange of giving and receiving. It's important to treat yourself with the same kindness and attention you would generously offer to those you care about. Remember, self-care and self-compassion are essential components of any meaningful connection.

Why hold back from giving yourself the same thoughtfulness and care you provide to loved ones?

You deserve to treat yourself with as much compassion and consideration as you offer others. This is necessary for maintaining a healthy relationship with oneself.

Take, for example, my brilliant private investor client Pippa, who completely upended her life in London because of her daughter's struggles with substance abuse and depression. While her affluent ex continues his life unchanged in another country, she is sacrificing everything she has to look after their child, who remains selfish and defiant.

This level of self-sacrifice, verging on martyrdom, prompts us to contemplate whether it's effective. Often, such extreme self-sacrifice falls short of yielding the desired results, instead resulting in personal imbalance and a perception of martyrdom. It serves as an important reminder of the significance of maintaining balance and preserving one's own identity while offering assistance to others.

Self-Compassion

We often find ourselves caught in the illusion that our sacrifices will be recognized or repaid. However, the concept of martyrdom is inherently unreciprocated. It represents an outdated and one-sided path that rarely leads to the rewards we envision. Certainly, it is instinctual to make sacrifices for your children. However, it is equally imperative to prioritize your own well-being and mindset to effectively support your children.

Pippa, my client, decided to leave her London residence and reside in a remote countryside location for a year. Despite her affluent status, she neglected her own personal well-being. As a result, she experienced increased feelings of unworthiness. Our discussions surrounding self-care did not align with the actual choices she made, which shed light on a more profound underlying issue—lack of self-compassion.

Pippa needed to acknowledge that performing miracles was beyond her capabilities. Her top priority should have been self-care and entrusting professionals to address her loved one's issues. While her concern for her child's forgiveness for removing her from the temptation of the city was valid, it should not overshadow the imperative of seeking professional intervention for her well-being.

Her decision to embrace martyrdom instead of self-preservation was bewildering to me.

Sometimes we rush to aid others in distress, yet when we

suffer, we often endure it silently. Allowing others to help carry our burdens is as vital as our willingness to help them.

Express Yourself

People are not mind readers. We do not learn by osmosis. If you are struggling or need something, your duty to yourself is to speak up. If others are unaware of your needs, they won't be able to help you. Asking for assistance isn't about feeling guilty or appearing needy; it's about being practical and efficient.

Recognize your emotions and speak your mind. Avoid bottling up your emotions until they reach a breaking point, leading to an explosive outburst. This can leave others perplexed, as they may be unaware of any underlying issues from your choice to remain silent, believing it to be the right course of action.

Perhaps you've held on to the notion that sharing your problems is unwelcome or that you must face them alone. Yet, as humans, we yearn for connection, and solitude isn't always the solution.

Emotional isolation often exacerbates issues, changing manageable problems into insurmountable obstacles. Be sure to express your needs and actively seek empathy, understanding, or simply a compassionate listener. It's important for your mental health.

Suppressing emotions can result in a mental breakdown,

Self-Compassion

an accumulation of detrimental energy that hinders growth and severs the essential connections we crave for a harmonious existence. Yes, societal norms amplify the challenge of self-expression for women. We are frequently conditioned to bear the weight of life's burdens silently. We're often expected to be silent, compliant, and uncomplaining.

While men have traditionally been seen as the primary financial providers, this perspective often overlooks the diverse and vital roles that women also fulfill. Women excel in nurturing, contributing financially, and managing household responsibilities. This stark dichotomy raises questions about how such an imbalanced dynamic became the norm. In reality, women navigate life's complexities far beyond what is typically acknowledged. And as they navigate family and workplace, they need to learn to speak up about their own needs—and sometimes the needs of others too.

We must raise our voices, break free from perpetuating this cycle of women as compliant and secondary to men. And as we do, we can start to redefine societal norms.

So speak up and speak out. Assert the true value of our contributions in every aspect of life. More importantly, silence leads to a life of regrets and unfulfilled potential. Life is too precious to be clouded by unspoken words and unacknowledged struggles.

Eliminate Energy Drainers

People who consistently take without reciprocating are akin to energy-draining leeches. They monopolize your thoughts with their problems, hindering your ability to prioritize self-care. As mentioned previously regarding energy vampires, the time has come to sever ties with these energy vampires and reclaim your vitality.

Procrastination can be a significant drain on your energy, too, especially when it comes to tasks and responsibilities. These unfinished items loom over you like a dark cloud, infiltrating your thoughts, dreams, and conscience, leaving you burdened with guilt.

Embrace commitment to completing your tasks. Streamline your life and your to-do list, freeing yourself from unnecessary burdens.

But you need to remain balanced. Yes, stop procrastinating. But avoid stretching yourself too thin. Consistently pushing yourself to the limit to meet those deadlines only leads to exhaustion. While youth may give the illusion of resilience, it can still be a deceiving snare.

I caution my talented, ambitious twenty-eight-year-old daughter, "Listen to your body. When it screams for rest, don't ignore it."

Frequently, we exhaust our own energy by neglecting to set boundaries or permitting others to ignore them. This issue becomes even more complex when we fail to uphold our promises. The weight of unfinished tasks or unmet obligations burdens us, depleting our energy and giving rise to the "should have, could have, would have" syndrome.

Set realistic goals when you are attacking these energy drains. Understand your capabilities and respect your limitations. It's one thing to push yourself, but quite another to know when enough is enough.

Treat Yourself

The guilt of treating yourself to something is real, especially when it feels like you are forgoing responsibilities.

I spoke about this earlier in the chapter, and it's important for me to underline: You need to treat yourself. In fact, if you embrace abundance, abundance follows.

Knowing your limits and occasionally stepping beyond them to indulge yourself can be liberating. Do not let guilt negate the pleasure of a well-deserved treat. Embrace the belief, "What I spend will return to me."

That is the energy you need to attract. If engaging in self-care feels overwhelming, it ceases to be a treat and becomes a burden. Just as you acknowledge the hard work of others, your own efforts deserve equal, if not greater, recognition.

This mindset transformation changes how we view rewarding ourselves. Instead of it being a stressful task, it becomes a well-deserved celebration of our accomplishments. By rewarding ourselves, we acknowledge and honor the effort we have invested in our journey.

Rose's Story

Rose's tale is one that honored too much work and not enough reward.

I got to know Rose at my Tune Out, Tune In retreat for high-achieving women. She first heard about the retreat when I spoke at an event for Chief, a women's leadership organization. After the talk, she approached me, requested more information, and signed up during the first week of registration. There was an urgency in her demeanor that suggested she truly needed time to reflect on her life.

Rose crafted her life around ambition, determined to become a key player at Amazon. She decided to forgo marriage and children, diving headfirst into climbing the corporate ladder and embracing ever-bigger challenges. "It's not a place that you get the job and then prove yourself. You do the job one to two years before you're given the promotion or the level. It's reversed in the sense that you're killing yourself at the next level; then they kept moving the finish line of what it looks like from the promotion level."[21] Her career success became a defining part of her identity, even beyond the office walls.

But this relentless drive tested her mental and physical limits, pushing her to compromise her boundaries. She took on roles that didn't deliver the financial rewards or more prestigious titles she had been promised. Eventually, Rose realized her sacrifices weren't paying off as she had expected or been assured by her superiors.

Rose encountered the challenges that many women routinely face in the business world. "Women were getting promoted at a slower rate than men, particularly at senior levels. We're judged on performance, not potential." Classic.

During the COVID-19 era, Rose spearheaded a team of 250 stakeholders across seven countries, orchestrating a major recovery plan and building services from scratch. Despite her immense responsibilities and achievements, she received little more than a "thatta girl" as recognition and watched as a major promotion she deserved went to a male colleague. This chapter

---

21 Rose, interview by the author, October 1, 2024, London. All quotations from Rose in this chapter come from this interview.

in her career was a whirlwind of confusion and frustration, highlighting the challenges she faced in an often-unequal playing field.

"I was chasing something that wasn't going to happen. I stayed too long. It took me at least twelve months to get that the writing on the wall wasn't going to change." An informal mentor, another woman in a position of power, took Rose aside and told her she wasn't on the promotion track. "She sat me down and was really direct with me; it was amazing. She said, 'Listen, I don't agree with how it's going, but they're not going to give it to you. So you've got to move on.'"

Discovering that her hard work wouldn't pay off was a tough pill to swallow, leaving Rose grappling with disappointment and frustration. "I was super drained, pissed, went through the stages of depression, of grief, anger, denial, about what I was going through in terms of both work and personal life. . . . I didn't do a good job of assigning boundaries, and I lost time. I lost peace of mind. I needed to make a change."

Rose was unaware of the heavy toll stress was taking on her until it was almost too late. Despite being vaccinated twice, she contracted COVID-19, which led to a terrifying stint in the ICU and a brush with death. This traumatic experience forced her to reassess her life.

Upon recovery, she was offered an exciting global role at

Amazon, not in the warehouse sector but in the HR department, specifically focusing on DEI—a field Rose was passionate about. With newfound clarity on her boundaries and personal definition of success in the tech world, she dove in headfirst.

However, once again, she overlooked the signs of stress and burnout. Her global position demanded long hours, often starting at 7 a.m. and stretching until 9 p.m. This role introduced Rose to another new challenge many White people never face: being the only person of their race in the room. While her Black colleagues in senior positions had long adjusted to the discomfort of being the minority, for Rose, it was a new hurdle. She respected their resilience, but that understanding didn't make her journey any easier.

After discovering she was once again passed over for a big promotion, Rose realized that Amazon would always prioritize their interests over hers. She saw her situation as a toxic relationship that desperately needed to end.

"I think I was being dishonest with myself about the process and what it was going to give me as an outcome. I'd been there for so long, I was scared to think about life outside because I had used the protective blanket of that company for so long. However, I did have an amazing career. . . . I never went backward. Then all the tech layoffs started happening; I didn't feel comfortable letting go of the safety blanket."

THE QUIET BURN

In November 2023, Rose boldly discarded that false crutch. She redefined her worth beyond the confines of business and stopped letting others dictate her identity. By reclaiming her power, she took charge of her decisions and held herself accountable. Rose also carved out time to celebrate personal achievements, rewarding herself with newfound accomplishments. "I used a lot of the time to make up for things that I had been missing, in terms of time with family and time to do things I really love. I got my [British] citizenship, doing some basic life admin, just doing things I wanted to do that I hadn't done. I went on the retreat. I'd never invested in myself, really thinking about what next steps could look like for me and opening doors to what was possible."

Eager to embrace the future, Rose decided to set her sights on the horizon and move forward with determination. "It's ultimately just looking at the positives of it, knowing what I learned about it and moving on, because if you keep holding on to it, it's just going to haunt you. Time is the only gift I can give myself right now, and I actively made that choice to give myself time."

The way you treat yourself communicates a powerful message not only to others but, most importantly, to yourself.

You are worthy of good things. Go ahead and knock yourself

out on occasion! Do something special for yourself, and don't regret it.

Just do it.

I Deserve

Given the constant experience of being undervalued, particularly in the face of systemic biases and societal pressures that affect women, it becomes effortless to internalize a feeling of inadequacy and unworthiness.

Shedding this deeply ingrained belief is a formidable challenge. While we may outwardly declare, "I deserve this," inwardly, doubts still linger about how we earned the opportunity or reward. We can't overcome our feelings of unworthiness.

Some individuals even delve into cynicism, harboring suspicions that every opportunity comes with hidden motives, pondering what we are expected to reciprocate. This skepticism complicates our path toward self-acceptance and acknowledging our inherent worth.

The exodus of women from corporate environments, driven by a persistent lack of acknowledgment and compensation, presents a troubling reality. The workplace needs us! Yet maintaining a belief in our own worth becomes challenging when societal structures and workplace cultures neglect to provide the validation and support we need.

However, even in the face of these obstacles, hope persists. I firmly believe in the transformative power of a united voice, the strength found in sisterhood. Within a community that actively supports and validates one another, we can create a ripple effect of positive change.

This begins with nurturing an individual sense of self-worth. Confidence and positive outlook are not just personal traits, they are communal forces that inspire.

Your mere presence, exuding self-assurance and a proactive stance, possesses the power to ignite change in any setting. When you radiate confidence, it resonates with others. Such positivity is magnetic, drawing people in and compelling them to engage with and emulate this energy.

This is not just self-empowerment. This is setting a precedent. By fostering this, we create a space where the notion of "sharing in energy" becomes a reality.

Remember: Confidence is contagious. There is no one more deserving of your own rescue than yourself. You are invaluable, not just to others but, crucially, to your own existence.

Embracing your best self requires a firm belief in your worthiness. It can only begin from within you.

Prioritizing your needs is not just for your own benefit;

when you prioritize yourself, it ultimately uplifts everyone around you. By extending compassion to yourself, tuning in to your inner voice, trusting your instincts, and making choices that are right for you, you can change the world—one person at a time.

PART THREE

A Phoenix Rises from the Ashes

CHAPTER 8

Rebirth

When you play with fire, you get burned. That's the truth. And depending on the degree of the burn, it could take a short time or a very long time to recover.

However, most of the time we can recover. And it is a process—of courage, confidence, healing, and really believing that there's light on the other side.

I can't give you confidence. It doesn't come in a gift box. It comes from within. And there are a lot of elements involved in that. It starts with understanding exactly what confidence is: a combination of self-esteem, self-respect and confidence itself—the ability to front. They're all intertwined, but let's separate them for the purpose of clarity.

Self-confidence is your belief in yourself and your abilities. Naturally, that can change depending on your situation. It's normal to feel quite self-assured when you know something like the back of your hand. But when you are flying by the seat of your pants, you're probably not going to feel terribly confident. That's a no brainer. Self-esteem is about appreciating and valuing yourself. Your self-esteem evolves and changes as the result of your life experiences and interactions with other people.

There are two components of self-esteem: the unwavering belief in your own worth and the positive outlook that's called self-respect. It's reflected as a positive outlook where we believe it's our right to be happy and live a fulfilling life, pursuing worthy endeavors. When you have deep self-esteem, expressing your desires, thoughts, and needs is vital to your happiness.

Then there's self-efficacy. Self-efficacy refers to the confidence we have in our ability to learn, think, and acquire new skills necessary for achieving success. It's closely linked to our sense of control over our lives and contributes to our overall psychological well-being. Feeling secure in both facets of confidence is key to a successful recovery from burnout.

Healthy self-esteem allows you to examine things that have gone wrong in your life, with a desire for clarification and understanding. It gives you the ability to be objective about mistakes, consider what went wrong, and as a result, to do better next time. Although you might feel disappointed by that loss, you don't feel diminished as a person. You are able to pick yourself up, dust yourself off, and get back in the game, and that's what you need to do when you're recovering from burnout.

Be Proactive

So how do we turn low self-esteem into self-respect? Well, you've got to be proactive. Different things work for different people at different times, and you should only try the things that you're absolutely comfortable with. If you've been doing the exercises I prescribe throughout this book, you should have more self-awareness of your values, beliefs, and what makes you happy. Moving forward I encourage you to keep a journal about the good, bad, and ugly things that happen to you each week.

Challenge unkind thoughts about yourself. Do not allow yourself to turn on your autopilot. Autopilot is a mode that allows you to dull your senses, say yes when you mean no, compromise your personal boundaries, and put yourself down when you've been down or been kicked down. Remember, you need to maintain a heightened awareness to smell the smoke that turns into the fire that becomes burnout.

Make it a habit to recognize the positives in every facet of your life. Staying positive is incredibly important to your comeback. Though it may feel uncomfortable, stand in front of a mirror every morning and night and use the mantra I shared earlier: I am a force for good, I am a force for change, I am force to be reckoned with. Start off softly, and increase the passion and volume in your voice with each repetition. By the third time, you should be feeling it in your bones! Say it loud and say it proud!

Be assertive. I know it's difficult if you're not used to it, but don't agree to too many things just to please others. In other words, don't go along to get along, because that becomes an energy drainer for none other than you. So pause, take a breath, and think how you feel before agreeing to do something you don't want to do.

Avoid comparing yourself to others, because you are not like anyone else. You are your unique self. Limit how much time you spend on social media or in online communities. What people choose to share about their lives isn't always the full picture, and it will definitely warp your perspective.

With an understanding of self-esteem, let's look at the confidence factor of this equation.

Confidence is a game changer. It equips you with the power to navigate complex issues with finesse, supercharge your communication skills, and find joy in your work and in your life. Embrace feedback gracefully and unlock your potential as an exceptional person and an exceptional leader. With confidence you can exceed your potential and watch your success soar.

Lesley's Story

Everyone experiences crises of confidence at points in their lives, so you're not alone. Let me tell you about one of my brilliant clients, Lesley, who suffered severe burnout, hit rock bottom, lost all of her confidence, and is now building back better.

In the competitive landscape of the tech industry, women often face unique challenges that can impede their professional growth and personal well-being. Lesley, once a high-powered female executive who worked for three industry giants, including Meta and TikTok, experienced these challenges firsthand. She struggled with discrimination, underpayment, and a toxic work culture that eventually led to severe burnout.

Lesley's story is a poignant example of the systemic issues faced by women in tech. Despite her impressive credentials and high-ranking positions, she was consistently undermined, underpaid, and uncredited for her work. The pervasive "bro" culture made her feel like an outsider—for example, if she didn't conform to the campus dress code of chinos and Patagonia gear.

Her mental and physical health deteriorated as she was expected to be available 24/7. "I have never had a job impact my mental health the way that my last tech job did," she said.[22] Even during vacations in remote locations, she was expected to answer calls and emails, which contributed to her increasing sense of dread and disengagement.

Over the course of her last year in big tech, she gained forty pounds and had to start antidepression medication because of the overwhelming stress and toxic environment. This led her to leave not only her job but also America, seeking refuge in Paris. "Best decision I've ever made was leaving San Francisco and moving to Paris. Second best decision I've ever made is getting out of tech," she shared.

Unfortunately, her experience is not unique. Statistics reveal that women are underrepresented at all levels of tech, particularly in management. And 72 percent of women in tech have faced sexism, including pay disparities and skill questioning. Discrimination is even more pronounced for Black and minoritized women, with nearly three in four experiencing racism at work. Women in tech often face imposter syndrome, with 66 percent of female entrepreneurs finding it challenging to secure

---

22   Lesley, interview by the author, September 3, 2024, Paris, France. All quotations from Lesley in this chapter come from this interview.

business funding. Additionally, the scarcity of female role models can deter women from entering tech careers.[23]

Addressing burnout, career dissatisfaction, and crises of confidence and self-esteem requires a multifaceted approach. We began by exploring the "why" behind Lesley's experiences:

- Why did she ignore warning signs of mistreatment? She was motivated by the wrong things—money and status.

- Why was she afraid to speak up? She lacked a support system, sponsor, or other women who would stand up with her and for her.

- Why did she accept tasks outside her job description? She wanted to appear to be a team player even though she often felt apart from the team. Furthermore, she mistakenly thought she would be rewarded if she kept her head down and worked hard.

- Why did she allow others to trample her boundaries? She simply lost herself. Life conditions women to put their needs last. For Lesley, the hamster wheel became routine; she couldn't stop spinning.

---

23 "System Update: Addressing the Gender Gap in Tech," Fawcett, October 30, 2023, https://www.fawcettsociety.org.uk/system-update-addressing-the-gender-gap-in-tech-report; Raija Haughn, "Closing the Gap: How to Overcome Obstacles as a Female Entrepreneur," *Yahoo! Finance*, June 13, 2023, https://finance.yahoo.com/news/closing-gap-overcome-obstacles-female-150909434.html; Maria Lehtman, "The Importance of Role Models for Women in Technology," Orange Business, March 5, 2024, https://www.orange-business.com/en/blogs/importance-role-models-women-technology.

Understanding the answers to these questions helped Lesley gain self-awareness and ensured she wouldn't repeat the same mistakes.

Next, we tackled her lack of motivation. Despite her innate ambition, Lesley's terrible experience had convinced her that she wanted only low-stakes jobs. We revisited her core values, beliefs, passions, and purpose. This deep introspection rekindled her drive, leading to a pivotal realization during one of our sessions: Perhaps her intuition was telling her to close the door on traditional tech roles.

Rebuilding confidence and tackling imposter syndrome was also crucial. We pinpointed her five signature strengths, such as developing people, being tech-savvy, and appreciating diversity, with specific examples illustrating her excellence in these areas. Being aware of these strengths, alongside her achievements, helps reduce imposter syndrome and enhances confidence with facts and data—two elements that are hard to dismiss.

We explored her transferable skills and brainstormed potential career paths in AI tech and privacy, luxury industry consulting, government policy, and think tank work. By leveraging her extensive tech knowledge, she could transition into roles that aligned with her values and strengths.

Rebirth

After working together intensely, the transformation was palpable. Now, Lesley feels more alive, confident, self-aware, and assured. She recognizes and owns her value, which has opened new and exciting doors outside traditional tech roles.

While this is a journey in progress, the results are promising:

- Increased self-awareness and confidence
- Identification of new career paths aligned with her values and strengths
- A renewed sense of purpose and motivation

Lesley's story serves as a powerful reminder that you can rise from the ashes. You can reframe disappointing experiences and move forward with an understanding of how you got there in the first place and how you will never let yourself go there again. *Can I get an amen!*

We have choices in life. You can choose not to perpetuate the cycle of negative behaviors, you can choose to exercise the power of positive thinking, and you can make the decision to prioritize your needs and break that cycle that perpetuates negative thinking, negative expectations for the future, and discourages you from trying. That will only lead to disappointing outcomes.

Finding confidence can be more difficult for some people.

Research shows that between 25 and 50 percent of personality traits are linked to confidence, and those traits are inherited.[24] Furthermore, women are socialized to worry more about how they're perceived, and therefore we take fewer risks, which in turn has a negative impact on confidence. Women also worry more about what other people think. Personally, I think it's nice to be liked, and loved. But if you don't like or love me, I'm all right with that, because I love myself—and that is the greatest love of all.

I got to that point, and so can you.

I've said it before and I will continue to say it: There's no such thing as perfection. Striving for the impossible will only knock your confidence. Perfectionism is a form of faulty thinking that contributes to low self-confidence, keeping one from doing things that they really value.

Reasons You May Have Low Self-Esteem

We can start with the world at large. We live in a world that has been dominated by leaders who try to control us by fear and hate. It's hard to find confidence with the likes of Trump, Putin,

---

[24] Randi L. Vogt, Anqing Zheng, Daniel A. Briley, Margherita Malanchini, K. Paige Harden, and Elliot M. Tucker-Drob, "Genetic and Environmental Factors of Non-Ability-Based Confidence," *Social Psychological and Personality Science* 13, no. 3 (September 2021), https://www.ncbi.nlm.nih.gov/pmc/articles/PMC11244733/.

Rebirth

Ahmadzai, Jinping, Castro, Jong-un, Mohamud, and dozens of other men telling women we're expendable, that we should be seen more than heard, and that we are not in control of our own bodies. If that doesn't deteriorate your confidence, add toxic social media to the mix.

The media messages we are bombarded with every day make us feel lacking. Businesses push us to buy into products that start with the catalyst of making you feel bad about yourself. They trigger people to consider problems with your body, with your mind, and with your life that you may have never noticed otherwise.

You may also have low confidence because of anxiety and depression. They go hand in hand with self-confidence issues. Sometimes these conditions are transient and can be overcome with mindful behavior, exercise, time out, eating properly, and practicing good mental hygiene. If anxiety and depression are persistent and confidence is consistently suffering, it's time to reach out for help. Reaching out for help is a show of strength, not shame. When you feel low, get help even if it means pushing yourself out of your comfort zone.

When you look at the confidence chain, it starts out with a happening, something that occurred, and self-doubt reared its head. Say for example you returned to work before you had completely recovered from burnout, something many people do. Stepping into the office immediately triggers negative thoughts, causing emotional anxiety. This triggers your body to go into fight-or-flight mode, resulting in panic, self-doubt, and the return of that pesky confidence crisis.

We become aware of our level of confidence through an event that triggers a chain reaction in us. According to cognitive behavioral therapy (CBT), which triggers how we react and think, it is not the event itself, but how we interpret it that causes us anguish, and this will depend on our level of self-esteem.

Have you ever been in a situation when you had a performance review where your manager made several brilliant observations about your achievements over the year and perhaps some things you could improve on? Then after that review, the points your mind focused on the most were not the many things you excelled in, but the two things you could have done better?

Despite the overall positive review, if your self-confidence is low, it's likely you'll think the year has been a failure. This experience and your reactions are interconnected and will result in a negative outcome. You physically may feel tense, have a faster heartbeat and defensive position—arms closed and your body feeling the weight of disappointment. Your behavior will reflect that inner turmoil. All these things that go on within you are expressed through your behavior, your physical actions.

However, if you have confidence and are thinking positively, then you may look at that feedback for what it's worth. You will be pleased about the positives and take on board the things you can improve. Confidence helps you look at the big picture, to gain perspective and clarity, helping you to understand that constructive criticism does not equate to failure, embarrassment, or personal/professional disappointment. You may even feel excited about the prospect of finding out how to do something better and embrace the challenge.

You can break the negative self-confidence chain. You can break any negative behavior cycle by the way you interpret an event, how you think, or how you react. The lesson here is to be self-aware in situations that can produce negative recall, which damages your confidence and self-esteem. At this point in the book, your toolbox is full of ways to see situations for what they are, value your worth, and to keep calm, cool, and collected in daunting situations.

Relight Your Fire, the Right Way

Returning to a workplace that may have once seemed hostile, where you felt overwhelmed and undervalued, is not the best idea. You may feel compelled for financial or personal reasons to return to the scene of the crime, but I ask you to rethink this. Remember, you have choices. Sometimes it means starting small to grow something big. But trust me, it's worth building a better, more balanced life going forward.

When you decide it's time to make that comeback, be prepared to put your needs first, because you know what it feels like to play with fire and get burned. Ouch!!! These steps will help you ease you back onto your career path:

- Be prepared to ask for what you want. It will make you feel confident.

- Ask to attend professional development training. This will improve your skills and boost your confidence. Be specific about the training you want to do—something women are reluctant to do. Men are naturally given learning and development to build on their potential and hone their expertise, whereas women are more likely to have to ask for L&D opportunities. Remember what I said earlier: Don't ask, don't get. Curiosity is the number one leadership quality, and developing new skills and continuing your education will have a lasting impact on your confidence.

- Dress for success. Yes, in the big picture, dressing well is near the bottom of the top ten things successful people do. Nonetheless, in my experience when I dress myself in a way that makes me feel comfortable and confident, I shine. So consider your wardrobe and align your appearance with your professional goals. Remember, appearance counts for 93 percent of first impressions, only 7 percent is about what you say. Dressing professionally can boost your confidence in job performance and interactions with colleagues, and certainly with your leaders.

- Leave your comfort zone. Stepping outside of your comfort zone is a powerful way to gain confidence. Make yourself visible in meetings. Volunteer to solve problems when time permits. Don't be afraid to flex your expertise by giving presentations or asking for the glory jobs over the housekeeping jobs. Emphasize your skills rather than worrying about mistakes and embarrassments. Stepping out of your comfort zone will open new opportunities for advancement.

- Emulate confidence. Observe successful people or those who exude confidence. Learn from their mannerisms and their terms, and apply those strategies to develop your own confidence.

- Set goals for yourself; establish short-term and long-term goals. These goals can shift your perception of strength and success. Focus on developing new skills and overall capacity, and break goals into smaller objectives. Start with a slow build. Celebrate each small success as you work toward your larger goal and recognize that effective strategies contribute to your growth and boost your confidence. Always focus on your strengths. We all have a superpower, and we all have signature strengths. Honor them. Create your list of strengths, abilities, and achievements and make a habit of reviewing them daily for a boost in confidence. And remember, eliminate negative language.

- Ask questions. Successful people ask questions without the worry of sounding foolish. Boost your confidence by asking questions and being assertive in learning. Make it a habit to seek answers during team meetings, planning sessions, and conferences. Clarify information, show initiative, and make clear your desire for direction. When you do this, confidence and self-worth will grow. So grow. Additionally, offering to ask questions can help alleviate anxieties of coworkers and build their confidence about you.

- Continually assess how you perceive yourself. Remind yourself to do things differently on this side of your journey, the side of light and recovery. Avoid excessive self-criticism and self-doubt; practice self-affirming techniques. Focus on past successes, which will encourage you to build new ones. Acknowledge career improvements and praise yourself abundantly when projects are completed successfully or exceed expectations. Own your glory.

- Finally, learn from your mistakes. Mistakes are part of improvement and goal setting. Analyze mistakes and use them as opportunities to learn and grow. Accept failure as a part of life. We cannot achieve success without failure. Reflect on errors, identify their causes, and correct them to build yourself a better future.

The Power of Self-Belief

Remember, if you don't believe in yourself, then who will? Why do our thoughts and convictions have such a consequential hold on us? It's the courage they give us to dream, to take risks, to wonder, to experience anything that enhances the human spirit. Psychologist James Maddux concluded that self-belief is one of the most significant factors in success.[25] Of course you need skills, strategy, resources, determination, and luck to achieve our goals, but never underestimate the power of self-belief. Countless research studies have shown that the power of self-belief

---

25   Marianna Pogosyan, "The Power of Believing in Yourself," *Psychology Today*, July 22, 2022, https://www.psychologytoday.com/intl/blog/between-cultures/202207/the-power-believing-in-yourself.

helps us to achieve our goals, combat stress more effectively, and promote health-conscious behavior.

One of the key elements of self-belief is self-regulation. Self-regulation will stop you from repeating the behaviors that caused you to burn out in the first place. It is a potent tool that steers our behaviors, thoughts, and emotions toward achieving our goals and desired outcomes. By reflecting on past experiences, we form expectations about future events. Imagine it as a dynamic process where networks, factors, and predictions continuously interact and evolve. Self-regulation is a tool for self-salvation. It is key to maintaining a successful, balanced life.

Achieving success in self-regulation is within your reach. It involves developing strong self-efficacy beliefs, setting meaningful goals, integrating feedback, and adapting performance strategies. Mastering these skills is essential for psychological well-being, providing a sense of control over a person's life. Embrace this ability on your journey toward empowerment. You've got this.

Start with self-awareness. Reflecting on my past, as I said previously, I foolishly ignored signs of stress and anxiety that took a toll on my lower back, eventually leading to the deterioration of two discs. That was a hard lesson learned. Now I stand tall—supported by a titanium cage!

Recovering from my surgeries was a grueling journey,

numbing my nerves with painkillers and leaving me in a zombie state for nearly six long months. Now, five years later, I've transformed that experience into a heightened awareness of stress, anxiety, and circuit overload. Any hint of pain activates my internal alarm, triggering my self-regulation and reinforcing my belief in maintaining my boundaries and respecting my well-being. I've learned that I don't need to sacrifice myself to achieve success. This realization is my guiding principle, empowering me to live up to my potential and achieve my goals without breaking my back. This is my truth, and I'm unapologetically embracing it.

Building Back with Resilience: Adeya's Story

Resilience is more than just enduring tough times—it's our power to rise above adversity, adapt to change, and recover from setbacks, both physically and emotionally. Picture it as your mental muscle, ready to flex when life challenges you.

Resilience is not one-size-fits-all. It's a dynamic blend of awareness, adaptation, action, and acceptance. Understanding these facets empowers you to tap into your inner strength and overcome burnout.

In 2024 I co-facilitated a three-day leadership summit in London for women from high-profile companies in both the private and the public sector. From employees of medical insurer Bupa, to energy giant E-ON, to the Ministry of Defence, to the Department of Water and Power, nearly all of these women had experienced some degree of burnout and were looking for ways to combat the symptoms before they were suffocated with responsibilities. It was then that I met consultant clinical psychologist Adeya. She was invited to address the attendees about resilience. What the audience related to was her forthright authenticity about what it means to be resilient and what it means to be resilient as a Black career woman, mother, and wife in the world today.

As a child, Adeya's world shifted when her family moved from Nigeria to a predominantly White neighborhood in the UK. Suddenly, she found herself one of few persons of her background amid unfamiliar surroundings. This became her new normal, and through her formative school years, with resilience, she mastered the art of navigating this constant reality.

"I was always used to being the minority, very much in the minority. So, when I started my doctorate in 2004, I was the only Black person on the course of forty-two people. I wasn't the only minority, but I was the only Black person, and obviously Black female. And I always felt different. It just was the way it was."[26]

---

26   Adeya, interview by the author, October 12, 2024, London. All quotations from Adeya in this chapter come from this interview.

Rebirth

Beyond feeling like the "other," she felt a strong drive to outshine everyone else. Many Black individuals and those from underrepresented communities feel the pressure to work twice as hard for the same success as their White counterparts. Driven by resilience and determination, they strive to break barriers and redefine success. "Being good is not good enough. You've got to be excellent with the spirit of excellence." Adeya excelled as she advanced through the ranks of the UK's National Health Service (NHS) as a clinical psychologist, a journey she initially took for granted. Over the years, her career flourished, culminating in a strategic leadership role after she returned from maternity leave. This new position focused on reducing waiting times for children's services at a trust within the NHS.

However, Adeya faced the challenge of managing various personalities and leadership styles, leading to friction among service managers over the project's vision and execution. As a seasoned NHS professional, Adeya believed she had a firm grasp on the service's ethos and values, particularly when it came to children's outcomes and service delivery. But she often faced jarring surprise from people not expecting a young Black woman in a role of authority. Her straightforward leadership style sometimes sparked skepticism about her capability as a leader, and older colleagues occasionally resented taking direction from someone younger. Where she once garnered respect for her work, she now faced unexpected disrespect, leaving her questioning the reasons behind this shift.

A few months into her role, her director presented Adeya with an exciting opportunity: a yearlong leadership course designed to prepare her for a board position. This chance marked a pivotal moment in her career. The NHS Leadership Academy course, specifically crafted for BAME (Black, Asian, and minority ethnic) staff, was a revelation for Adeya. For the first time, she was among peers with similar backgrounds, surrounded by talented and successful individuals. No longer the "only" one in the room, she found the experience to be truly transformative. "Well, it was not being a unicorn in the room. I was in a room with other people of color who were doing amazing things. And that was new—to sit in a room with so many of them."

The course prompted Adeya to reevaluate her perspective on how she was being treated at work. "I think for the first time as a Black woman, I realized that I was a Black woman in a very White organization. Of course, I'd known that, but it made me really want to pay attention. I was really having to think about this." She found herself in a whirlwind of self-doubt, questioning her abilities and her work. Was this harsh treatment just a part of leadership, an unavoidable aspect of the job? She wondered if the solution was simply to toughen up, to grow a thicker skin and manage the burn. Constantly receiving confusing and conflicting feedback from her peers and superiors prompted her to keep a journal chronicling the mistreatment she experienced at work.

"It was really baffling for me," she said, "the hostility that I was experiencing from them, and that translated into our team meetings, which were often very tense. I thought they were undermining me, or they were constantly questioning everything that I said."

Personally, Adeya was grappling with the grief of losing her mother while striving to remain strong for her husband and young children. "This was also life-changing. I had to learn to be in the world without her. I lost a huge part of my identity when I lost her."

Like many Black women encouraged to remain resilient despite intense pressures, Adeya persevered in the toxic NHS environment until it began taking a toll on her physical health. "It didn't feel safe. This wasn't feeling like a safe place. I was feeling incredibly anxious about making mistakes. I was feeling undermined. I was being shouted at, spoken very rudely to in meetings with other professionals in the room, baffled when people didn't speak up. It was very toxic. And even now, I still get anxiety as I speak."

Ultimately, Adeya reached her burning point. She emailed a detailed account of the abuses she had endured to the CEO, the chair of the NHS trust, and the head of HR, and stated, "I'm taking some sick time off, and I actually think this is trauma. This is a racist organization toward ethnic and minority staff."

Adeya embarked on a ten-week leave, a period marked by intense consultations with lawyers on both sides and the involvement of an independent investigator. Unsurprisingly, fear gripped her throughout this tumultuous time. "I was on the sofa for a week after I did it, paralyzed with fear that I had ruined my career, and I was never going to work again. I didn't know what was going to happen, but I just knew that I needed to not be there, and I needed to speak up."

Adeya embraced her strength and resilience, and her stand against injustice benefited not only herself but also her colleagues from minority backgrounds. Refusing a quiet settlement, she was committed to transforming how minorities were treated within the NHS. With a persuasive argument, she successfully convinced the NHS board to commission a review of the experiences of Black, Asian, and minority ethnic staff within the organization. "They put a lot of money into something that actually took place, and I was part of it. I was part of the interview process, the pitch, the tender process, the recruitment of the people that were going to do it, and on the steering group—as was the CEO. I never knew I could do such things. I also got a promotion. That's how I ended up becoming a consultant clinical psychologist. I couldn't believe I had gone from that broken person to that person who was going to hold a budget of 1.2 million and literally be fronting and leading something."

Adeya took the job to prove her skills, but in her mind, she was already planning her exit. She realized that the NHS wasn't where she belonged anymore—her chapter there had closed. With the right support, she was ready to embark on a journey toward a more fulfilling and balanced career. "I think support is key. Know your tribe. I've got my husband. I've got my friends who know me. And I think relationships are key, particularly outside of those situations. Just having people around you that can remind you of who you are, that's been essential. Also, therapy and coaching are relationships—they're relationships in a different form, but they are relationships."

Today, Adeya thrives as a self-employed professional, boosting her self-awareness, enhancing her well-being, and mastering the art of handling pressure with grace. "I know how to pace. I know when to say no, and I'm not fearful of saying no anymore. What's important is feeling that there's a balance in my life, that I am working enough to feel that I am fulfilled professionally but that I'm also here, able to be present with my family and to give them what they need. I have the time to prioritize my self-care, going to the gym, taking time off, and going away by myself. This point in my life is all about balance."

Cultivate Resilience

Awareness means embracing the truth of any situation; it empowers you to plan with precision and insight. Awareness means confronting reality head-on, not sugarcoating it with wishful thinking. It's your compass through life's challenges, helping you navigate with clarity and confidence.

Resilience is owning your strengths and acknowledging your weaknesses. Self-awareness is your key to making bold, intentional decisions about your capabilities and knowing when to seek support. It's about strategically pushing your limits and maximizing your potential.

You will need emotional and physical flexibility on the road to burnout recovery. Furthermore, adaptability is your superpower in a world that never stops changing. Whether it's a sudden career shift or an unexpected life event, being able to bend without breaking is essential to maintaining well-being. I have thrived by embracing change with resilience, and so can you.

Change is inevitable, and embracing it confidently is crucial. Through my journey, I've discovered that resilience and adaptability are essential for thriving in a dynamic world. My extensive experience in overcoming challenges has highlighted the importance of strength and self-belief.

Cultivating self-awareness and understanding others empowers you to proactively initiate change. When faced with unsustainable situations or opportunities for improvement, adaptability becomes an invaluable asset.

At times, changes occur beyond your control. Adaptability involves trusting that you'll access the necessary resources to navigate any challenges. It's about resilience amid uncertainty.

Conclusion

This book is your wake-up call to genuine self-awareness.

Do not simply close the book and revert to your previous habits. Instead, leverage it as a launchpad for transformative change.

Change what you don't like. Extinguish the fires. Eliminate the energy drainers. Establish clear boundaries.

When you prioritize self-care, you set an example for others to do the same. By nurturing yourself, you not only replenish your own well-being but also enhance your ability to give to others and excel in doing so.

We must acknowledge that our mission is to advocate for diversity, equity, and inclusion, all while prioritizing our well-being and avoiding undue burdens. Because it is time to even the odds.

If we aspire to be treated as equals and to reap the benefits of a diverse world, including diversity in influential positions, we must be prepared to engage in certain battles.

But this change will take serious work. Mastering the art of altering behavioral processes and breaking free from ingrained teachings requires effort. It's a process of reprogramming oneself. This book serves as just one piece of the puzzle in this transformative journey.

Change your mindset, and become more self-aware.

Recognize those early warning signs, those wisps of smoke, before they become a full-blown fire that consumes you. Smell the smoke before it turns to flames, and the flame burns you out.

When you reach the point where you confidently declare, "Enough is enough; no more of this nonsense," it becomes a transformative moment. It's liberating yourself from a burden that has weighed heavily on your shoulders.

Free yourself from the weight of imposed obligations, whether they are thrust on you or self-imposed. While it is undeniably rewarding to be valued by others, what truly matters is the inherent self-worth that resides within you.

You only have this one life; live it with zeal and give it your all, but not at the cost of self-respect.

I want you to face the unfiltered truth of the challenges we face as women and the additional burdens we carry. My hope is that this truth ignites genuine anger within you and prompts you to question, "Why do I tolerate this?" I want it to ignite that inner flame, the kind that propels change.

Conclusion

Recognize the power of sisterhood, for when we unite, we become an unstoppable force for good. Let our collective voices be heard, resonating with strength and demanding acknowledgment. Embrace the strength in unity, because together, we can create positive change.

Collectively, we have a resounding roar that demands attention. It refuses to be disregarded.

For every woman who starts seeing her worth, who understands her value, that is one more powerful voice added to our chorus. Together, that voice cannot be silenced or sidelined.

You are already enough.

Let go of the pursuit of perfection; it's an illusion. Instead, embrace what can and cannot be changed. Harness your strengths and avoid exhausting yourself for those who wouldn't do the same for you.

Life is a journey of reciprocity, yet too often in both professional and personal settings, we find ourselves giving more than we receive. Emotional intelligence has become a hot topic of conversation lately, but it's time to realign and recalibrate that intelligence. Let us strive for a harmonious balance, where our actions and interactions reflect the true essence of reciprocity.

Although both genders possess it equally, men tend to prioritize self-preservation, while women lean toward nurturing others and cultivating relationships. It is now time to strike a balance. Women need to embrace a bit more self-care and sprinkle in some self-promotion, all while maintaining our ability to connect with others.

Make yourself visible. No one notices a shrinking violet. It's time to step into the light, articulating our wants and needs boldly.

Playing it safe and avoiding risks can result in missed opportunities for growth and success. By staying within our comfort zones, we risk stagnation and the absence of progress or true fulfilment. Embracing the unknown and venturing outside of familiarity is where real joy and personal growth can be found.

Consider the precedent we set for our children, as they imitate our every move and gesture. I aspire for my daughter to embrace her ability to conquer any challenge while also cherishing her well-being, pursuing her passions, and recognizing the significance of her own happiness.

Wealth and success mean little if they leave you unfulfilled or burnt out. Strive for fulfilment, so your achievements bring genuine joy.

Rejecting the status quo, I advocate for change and demand respect. My circle includes only those who treat me right.

In the workplace, there is often a tendency to overlook the quiet yet highly competent individuals. These are the ones who silently tackle every task that comes their way, always ready with

Conclusion

a "yes" and a solution. They are the dependable types, although they may shy away from teamwork and prefer solitude.

The downside to this situation is that their diligent and unnoticed efforts seldom receive the acknowledgment they deserve, fostering a silent resentment. This suppressed discontent accumulates, possibly culminating in an emotional breaking point. However, it doesn't have to escalate to such extremes.

In challenging situations like this, it's wise to avoid releasing pent-up frustration explosively, as it won't contribute positively to your cause. Instead, take a moment to pause, calmly articulate your concerns, and assertively communicate them. This approach will be more effective and more conducive to achieving your desired resolution.

Confrontation is not a battle but a strategic discussion. Harness your righteous anger as a powerful tool to construct compelling arguments built on facts and logic rather than solely relying on emotions. By doing so, you can pave the way toward progress with clarity, conviction, and effectiveness.

Express your emotions openly and honestly. Make your case in a way that resonates with logic and reason.

Stand your ground through clear, assertive expression.

If all women were able to identify burnout at an early stage, confidently say no, and set clear boundaries, the realm of leadership would undergo a profound transformation. This shift would result in a fairer distribution of responsibilities, cultivating an emotionally intelligent, driven, yet compassionate atmosphere. There'd be less testosterone and far more balance.

It's time for another revolution.

Those of us on the brink of becoming burnt toast—those of us who are weary of enduring unequal treatment—we're the ones who will shake things up.

This is a rallying cry across all facets of our lives.

Your voice is your most powerful tool, and I want you to firmly say, "No more" now and mean it. Now is the moment to redistribute that overwhelming heap of responsibilities, entrusting them to those who are equally capable. Unload that weight.

Don't let fatigue be your norm. Strive for a rich life in balance and self-remembrance.

Reclaim the words "I" and "me" in your life; it's about overcoming the reluctance to put yourself first, often leading to being overlooked and sidelined.

Challenge the status quo, question authority, and don't shy away from breaking a few rules.

No more settling for less.

It's time to leave the Land of the Burnt.

About the Author

Lynn Blades is the inspirational founder of Legacy Leadership, an executive coaching consultancy committed to fostering a diverse and inclusive twenty-first-century workforce. A trailblazer in leadership coaching, Lynn empowers organizations to build cultures in which diverse talent thrives. As a distinguished Marshall Goldsmith executive coach with two decades of experience, Lynn has guided an extraordinary range of leaders—from C-suite executives to their teams—across industries such as finance, law, tech, media, marketing, and luxury. Her client roster includes globally recognized giants like Nike, KPMG, British Airways, and the Royal Bank of Canada, as well as influential names in media, including Sony Music, BBC, Warner Bros., and Universal Music Group. Lynn's impact doesn't stop at coaching. She champions the next generation of female leaders through regular three-day leadership summits and retreats inspiring confidence and capability.

Lynn's exceptional communication skills and signature can-do attitude were shaped by her successful career as an award-winning journalist. She worked with several international networks, including CBS, CNN, CNBC, BBC, ITV, Viacom, and Showtime Networks. Over the years, she excelled in developing, writing, presenting, and producing a wide range of content, from hard news to engaging entertainment programs.

Dedicated to shaping the future of leadership beyond her consultancy, Lynn serves on boards that amplify diverse talent. She is chair of the board of trustees for New Curators, a pioneering program that democratizes museum curation, and a trusted advisor to Creative Access.

With an unwavering belief in the power of inclusive leadership, Lynn is redefining not only what it means to lead but also who gets to lead, leaving an indelible impact on her clients.